STUFF

ART

ANTIQUES

ARTIFACTS

# CAREY MALONEY

# STUFF

## THE M (GROUP) INTERACTIVE GUIDE TO COLLECTING, DECORATING WITH, AND LEARNING ABOUT, WONDERFUL AND UNUSUAL THINGS

Editorial director: Suzanne Slesin
Design: Stafford Cliff
Managing editor: Regan Toews
Production: Dominick J. Santise, Jr.
Assistant editor: Deanna Kawitzky

POINTED LEAF PRESS, LLC.
WWW.POINTEDLEAFPRESS.COM

# I have found in life that the more you know, the more you like.

When I arrived in New York and started work at Christie's in the 1980s, I was a son of the Deep South—trust me, East Texas is as deep as it gets—and a lover of dark brown English furniture, Persian Serapi rugs, and Japanese Imari porcelain. Within months of exposure to the vast array of decorative and fine arts that pass through a great auction house, I was leaning more to French Directoire furniture, contemporary photography, and nervously skirting Art Deco—a reluctant suitor.

Architect Hermes Mallea, my husband and business partner, and I have had M (Group), an interior design and architecture firm based in Manhattan, for almost 30 years. Hermes and I are house people—something that is very Texan (me) and very Cuban (him). We love our own houses as well as other peoples', and when it comes to furnishing them, we're interested in a lot of different things—old and new, mass-produced, or one-of-a kind. We are happily obsessed. The psychiatric community must have a label for our sort of disorder.

Our clients hire M (Group) because we offer both disciplines under one roof: The architecture and the interior design are conceived and executed parallel to each other, with the right hand knowing exactly what the left is doing from the very beginning. Starting with our first client, a decorative arts genius at Christie's, we have had opportunities to decorate with and design around some seriously world-class stuff. The families we have worked for, those brave souls, have come to us with things they've collected with thought, care, and erudition; pieces they've inherited—the ones that got rich the old-fashioned way; and even treasures they've fished out of Manhattan dumpsters.

The common denominator with our gang is that they are all confident, informed, polite and, like us, house proud. These are people who are self-assured—or perhaps delusional—enough to fill their homes with the things they love, knowing that their personal alchemy of art and objects will all work together somehow. To ensure that it does indeed work, they bring M (Group) in to edit what they have, flesh out their collections with fantastic new things, and create an architectural setting with elegance, order and, if we have our way, glamour.

Since Hermes and I are interested and entertained by stuff, that's what I have focused on. There are design insights and ideas here, but no laundry list of decorating Dos and Don'ts. I concentrated on what we put in the houses: the furniture, art, and objects selected to make the rooms truly representative of our clients' interests and lives. Each project, from a large portfolio of stylistically and geographically diverse houses, reflects the personality of the owner—restrained or effusive, severely elegant, or slightly quirky.

*Stuff* is a primer on many of the subjects that interest us and our clients, and was written to inspire readers to explore new areas of collecting. The idea is for us all to learn something—myself happily included—about a lot of subjects, in the hope that maybe something will catch the reader's attention and inspire them to explore a particular subject in greater depth. I want to expand your horizons and inspire confidence. Hopefully, readers will learn a bit, ponder on their own rooms and possessions, and then go for it. Make a leap. Take a chance.

Because when it comes to finding great stuff, we have experience—and nothing builds confidence like experience. We've spent thirty years traveling far and wide, accumulating the best things for our clients and ourselves. We are worker bees and as such, are reluctant bottom fishers who have amassed a poor man's version of our rich clients' worlds. Good isn't necessarily expensive. It isn't how much you spend, it's how you spend.

As clients we've been shopping with, and who have learned the hard way, when I said: "Are you sure you don't want that, because I hate to be pushy but, full disclosure, we're buying it if you don't?" which translates to "Buy it!" Because a) It has to be a bargain if we can afford it, and b) you are going to be very sad when you see it on our wall looking like a million dollars and that thing you spent a million dollars on looks poor in comparison.

Since we have lots more information than we could share in this book, we decided to bring our monograph into the digital age. So dig a little deeper—each of our Topic pages has a link to a website accessible via your mobile device or computer. Download the Digimarc Discover app, point your mobile device at the page, and you will be taken to the websites of the great museums and the finest dealers. Interested in the slit gongs of Vanuatu? The *Stuff* website will show you the drums in use in a rare, filmed ceremony. Want to buy your own Protest Art? Our favorite ephemera dealers are in the link.

So, enough introductions. Please dive in. Hermes and I hope your design horizons will broaden and your world will expand.

1 *Carey Maloney;* 2 *Hermes Mallea;* 3 *Frankie;* 4 *Renaissance fountain in the courtyard of the Belnord apartment complex in Manhattan.*

# TOPICS

LEFT Bedlam reigns in a scene from director Frank Capra's 1938 movie *You Can't Take It With You.*

# We discovered the Hudson River, in Upstate New York, by chance, in our youth. It was a wonderful stroke of luck.

After a few summers of renting a charming eighteenth- or nineteenth century pile overlooking the river, we knew we loved the area between Rhinebeck, New York—twee—and Hudson, New York—not twee, and with a burgeoning antiques business—with Bard College close by, for a bit of youth and culture. We fantasized about being among the socially mythical River People, but never thought we'd make the real estate cut. And then one August day, we ran into the local broker who said there was a place five houses south of us that had just gone on the market on a site inside one of the large Livingston estates. "You are the only people I can think of who might 'get' it," he told us.

So twenty minutes later, we rode our bikes through the stone gates with their funereal bronze plaques that were straight out of a Mel Brooks movie—they could easily have read "Psychoneurotic Institute for the Very, Very Nervous." We biked for another quarter of a mile and I was loving the very splashy parvenu paved driveway. Arriving at the house, Hermes announced: "That is the most insulting recommendation I have ever heard. Is he crazy?!" There it was: red brick, red-stained cedar siding, stone veneer, and white-painted trim, sitting on a bald prairie. "The Casino," as it was known, was built in 1964 as a party house for a purported mobster (his Sing Sing stint is a giveaway) and it was the Brady Bunch on steroids, commanding a great site. Within moments of seeing the interior, with its eighteen-foot-high ceilings, the Tap Room, which comfortably seated twelve at a bar out of one of your snappier Days Inn, and a basement that clocked in at 5,500 square feet, I was sold. Hermes, the architect, was affronted. I was in love.

We bought it—no one else wanted it—and the first person we called was paint-and-color maestro Donald Kaufman, to come up with a camouflage color for the exterior. Once it was painted army green, the house receded back into the earth. We then attacked the interior—with its pine-beamed ceilings, walnut walls, and oak floors. I say "we," but the house was not up to Hermes' standards, so he boycotted all decision making. Score one for me.

Fifteen years later, it still isn't an architectural gem, but Hermes is resigned to his fate, and now we both love it. The rooms are few but big, and hopefully we've de-mobbed the interiors. The landscaping continues the camouflage concept and helps to make the house seem invisible. Until you step inside the front door, you think you are entering a little suburban ranch. You aren't.

Its sprawl works well for us alone, as well as for big groups. We've topped out at 350 people inside. There is only one small guest room, which suits us fine. It has all the creature comforts that your typical old Hudson River house doesn't have—modern bathrooms, steel construction, and central air-conditioning with a plethora of zones. Both the Texan, me, and the Cuban, Hermes, love that stuff. We don't go away for the weekend to huddle by a little fireplace—we go to laze on swings from India in front of a hearth that fits four-foot-long logs. It may not be very Columbia County, but it's very us.

OPPOSITE Our house faces west, with views over mown fields and across the Hudson River to the high peaks of the Catskill Mountain range. It sits very far back, and we love the Big Sky feel of our view.

OPPOSITE When we bought the house, the oversized blacktop driveway, sized for 1960s Fleetwoods, with its painted white curbs, came right up the concrete front steps. Kelly Varnell Virgona, Inc., landscape architects, a firm based in Bergenfield, New Jersey, brilliantly relocated the driveway and helped us place the house back into a native landscape. Every year, my mother sends us some very Southern caladiums bulbs from Texas. With annuals, more is more.

RIGHT By the front door, *Pegasus*, a sculpture cast in lead by the American artist Wheeler Williams in 1946, came to us via an auction at Sotheby's. Formerly in a Vanderbilt family garden, versions of the little winged horses also top tall columns at the Kansas City Zoo.

LEFT The porch, which opens off the living room and bar, has 15-foot-high ceilings at its peak, and wraps around the northwest corner of the house. In the summer, it becomes a sitting and dining room. The Moroccan rug came from New York dealer Doris Leslie Blau and was made in the 1950s. The wicker chairs were an impulse purchase in Kerala, India. We had sat in them at the hotel waiting for the car to take us to the airport, and asked the concierge to put a dozen—at 40 dollars apiece—in our container. What a happy impulse purchase!

25

# NAME: Moroccan rugs
# DATE: Nineteenth and twentieth centuries

When we want to tone down a fancy room, we throw a Moroccan rug into the mix. They are ethnic, graphic, and pale, with beautiful solid ivory-colored wool fields. The pale part is key. Tribal rugs are usually dark and earthy, since they are dependent on local dyes, not to mention the local cultural interpretations of what constitutes good taste. Quintessential Moroccan rugs are woven on small, portable looms by the semi-nomadic Berber women of the Beni Ouarain tribes in the Atlas Mountains of North Africa. Loosely woven with high pile to provide warmth, they were created for both personal use and internal trade. Until the middle of the twentieth century, these rural rugs were unknown outside of Morocco.

Berbers chillin' in the Sahara Desert, rugs strewn on the sands.

This camel, with an elaborately draped textile *howdah* (carriage), could be transporting a Muslim lady of high station in *purdah*, concealed from the prying eyes of men.

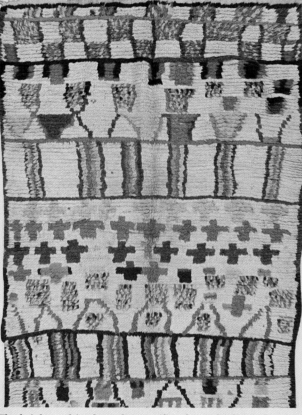

The bright multi-color palette unifies the multiple random geometric patterns on this mid-twentieth century runner.

Carpets dry in a village factory in the Ourika Valley in Morocco.

The Berbers have inhabited northern Africa for at least 3,000 years, with the majority now living in the mountains of Morocco. "Berber" is a variation on the Greek word for *barbaros*, or barbarian, which referred to anyone who didn't speak Greek—an example of semantic ethno-centrism that sums up the Greco-centric ancient world. The nomadic Berbers have a wonderful name for themselves—they are *Imazighen*, or free people.

As waves of foreign invaders occupied the coastal areas, the Berbers retreated to remote mountains and deserts, where they could preserve their languages and traditions. The graphic brown and black designs on off-white or natural-colored wool fields feel incredibly contemporary. Only vintage—not antique—Beni Ouarains can be found, and they are not very big: eight feet is their maximum width, as that is the size of their largest loom. Because they aren't very old or big, they are also not very expensive. The one we have is a great example from the 1950s. The pattern has a sort of message-from-outer-space quality. What are those wacky shapes and lines? The motifs have been passed down for generations—or are they just fooling us? Morocco is a large and very old country, and there are weaving traditions outside of the Beni Ouarain area that offer variations on the rural themes. The urban rugs were woven with outside influences from Africa and Arabia. A colorful palette of ochers and reds is typical and, very importantly for us, the looms on which these rugs were made were stationary and thus accommodated the production of large pieces. As much as we love the rural rugs, their small size limits us.

Chicago architect David Adler and his younger sister, decorator Frances Elkins, used a Moroccan runner on the incredibly chic staircase in the house of Mrs. Kersey Coates Reed in Lake Forest, Illinois, in 1932.

For more details about Moroccan rugs, please visit: www.mgroupstuff.com/moroccanrugs

**OPPOSITE In the front hall, the Morrocan rug can be seen through the glass-and-Lucite 1970s table. The large photograph of the California desert, by American artist Doug Hall, performs a double duty—both as artwork and as a "window," lightening a darkish corner.**

# NAME: Campaign furniture
# DATE: Seventeenth to twentieth century

The British East India Company arrived in India around 1600 and set in motion the British imperial system that would rule India until 1947. On the other side of the world, local hoi polloi sat on cushions on the floor—something that would never work for the Brits who needed Western-style furniture to reinforce their positions of authority and control. In their defense, they had grown up sitting on chairs. Given the long distances from England and the availability of high-quality hardwoods and craftsmen, European types of furniture quickly came to be manufactured locally, using samples and illustrations from back home.

This print from a watercolor of the line of march of a Bengal regiment in Scinde, India, in 1843, shows the parade of Indian bearers, camels, horses, British officers, and soldiers, moving what must have been tons of furniture and provisions.

A highly decorated Indian officer in the late nineteenth century combines his British uniform with traditional Indian headdress.

A campaign chest in two pieces plus a detachable base has flush handles and protective brass corner hardware.

Indian influences and aesthetics were welcomed and the exotic merged with the establishment. Since proper English ladies would never travel that far in the seventeenth and eighteenth centuries, officers of the British East India Company were encouraged to marry or keep Indian wives and concubines while they were posted away from home. The progeny from European fathers and Indian mothers were the true Anglo-Indians. This group intermarried and created a new demographic in India,

For the wealthy East India Company officers, furniture was more permanent and elaborate. This elegant ivory-inlaid bookcase would have been at home in Calcutta or London.

without caste or status in either the Indian or the British world. They became the great administrators of the colony, running the famously efficient railroads and postal systems, as well as the customs offices. The Anglo-Indians were the clerks of the empire and kept it growing. Our first encounter with the style was with nineteenth century Indian-made campaign furniture: simple masculine designs in mahogany and teak, with protective brass

elements on corners and feet, befitting the gentlemen officers' need for comfort and style. The chairs, chests, beds, and tables were designed to fold up or come apart to travel easily from one location to another. The functionality made for very elegant furniture for these conquerors on the move. The more elaborately carved residential pieces made for the ever-growing market of British expatriates who settled in India, and also for Indians who sought westernized interiors that reflected their desire to fit in with the British hierarchy, were our next interest. The designs took flight, and the latest European styles were overlaid or ornately carved with Mughal and Hindi flora and fauna, and inlaid with precious metals and ivory. Anglo-Indian design followed the route of western design, with Regency inspirations giving way to Victorian, then Edwardian, and finally to Moderne. Each style was subtly, or not so subtly, interpreted. On occasion, we have found some antique furniture in India, but as in many areas of collecting, the most desirable examples were exported to the West long ago.

For more details about Anglo-Indian furniture, please visit: www.mgroupstuff.com/angloindian

**OPPOSITE The old mahogany-and-glass retail display case was bought in India. Hermes filled it with four dioramas: From the bottom, St. Patrick expelling the snakes from Ireland; the Aztec god Quetzalcoatl; something I never quite understood; and Cerberus (also known as Frisky) at the Gates of Hell.**

RIGHT The living room is big and it filled up slowly—for the first few years it was empty, we jokingly called it Gallery Two. Any furniture we put in the space was dwarfed; so, channeling "Auntie Mame"'s fictional decorator, Yul Ulu, we decided on swings. For naps in front of the fireplace or for big rocking parties, they work for us. We had them made in Kerala from panels with Kama Sutra imagery. The low table is an Indian bed, and the painting is by British artist Graham Snow.

1 *Carpet, antique Ziegler Sultanabad, Persia, late nineteenth century.*

2 *South Indian teak bed, Kochi, Kerala, twentieth century.*

3 *Taxidermy penguin, Andy Warhol Collection, twentieth century.*

4 *Brass Indian water carrier, Mumbai, India, nineteenth century.*

5 *Late nineteenth century Nagaland, India, spear, John Stair Collection.*

6 *Graham Snow, born 1948, oil and glitter on panel.*

7 *Rhinoceros skull, twentieth century.*

8 *Architectural elements, South India, incorporated into new swings.*

9 *Ficus lyrata, also known as* Fiddle Leaf Fig. *We call it "that big-ass plant in the living room."*

10 *Rita Dee "Horse" driftwood from the Hudson River, New York, 1999.*

11 *Turkish* tula *weaving, angora wool, twentieth century.*

12 *Kerala, India, carved teakwood fishing boat prows, twentieth century.*

13 *Carved teak screens, India, twentieth century.*

14 *Elk horns, Wyoming, United States, twenty-first century.*

15 *Dioramas by Hermes, contemporary.*

LEFT The Genesee Beer billboard is a favorite thank you gift from one of our houseguests. He bought a stack of the posters at a local junk store, and we got one of the duplicates. Having had real art on the wall—actually huge paintings—we love the graphic, low-art feel of a highway billboard.

RIGHT There is a Noah's Ark's worth of life-sized animal sculptures in our house. I fell in love with this Japanese deer at Naga Antiques in New York. Each hair on his coat looks real, and his antlers are, in fact, real. The big glass containers flanking the fireplace are laboratory glass—I wonder what science lab they came from! The textile on the swing is a Turkish *tula*.

**NAME:** Taxidermy
**DATE:** Nineteenth and twentieth centuries

The first piece of taxidermy I had was a stuffed pug dog that I found in the 1980s on The King's Road in London. There he sat in a glass box, in the basement of the shop, with a tattered ribbon around his neck. I was poor and he was not an easy purchase. "Would he clear United States customs?" I wondered. "And what about shipping the glass box?" The shopkeeper clinched the deal with a major price reduction and a cheery, "Get the bloody thing out of my sight." The pug cleared customs in New York, the glass box was pitched, and he was christened Frisky. We feted his arrival for weeks.

The cabinet of curiosities that belonged to Ole Worm, 1588-1655, a Danish physician, featured taxidermy, minerals, fossils, and skeletons. Only the rich or the royal could assemble and maintain these private museum collections filled with oddities.

The *Musée de la Chasse et de la Nature* in Paris mounts wonderful exhibitions that spin their collections far beyond the basic hunt theme.

Every Renaissance ruler or aristocrat of learning had a *Wunderkammer*—a wonder room, or cabinet of curiosities—that included some examples of taxidermy. It was a home bestiary without the living beasts. This tradition continued as scholars and museums collected rare species, and the art of taxidermy became more acknowledged as a science. In eighteenth-century America, painter Charles Willson Peale opened his personal taxidermy museum in Philadelphia to the public. Later, his heirs sold the contents to circus entrepreneur P.T. Barnum. Barnum went on to exhibit one of the craziest faux creatures, the *Fee Jee Mermaid*—a combination of a baby monkey's head stuck onto a salmon carcass, with papier-mâché bits holding it together. People actually paid to see it. Carl Akeley is the father of modern taxidermy. He traveled with Theodore Roosevelt to Africa in 1909, where over

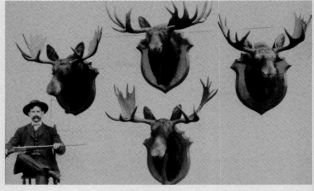

A late-nineteenth century photograph depicts a hunter and his four moose heads. His handlebar mustache is also a trophy.

A triptych of artist Andy Warhol, with his/our penguin, was taken in 1980 by photographer Jeffrey Rothstein.

11,500 animals were killed or captured for so-called scientific purposes. Upon his return, Akeley began his life's work, mounting the animals in naturalistic poses for the Field Museum in Chicago and the American Museum of Natural History in New York. He created the modern dioramas that we all love. We enjoy visiting natural history museums around the world. Even the grand European ones are always sort of funky. The ones further afield can be amazing. Mumbai's Chhatrapati Shivaji Maharaj Vastu Sangrahalaya, formerly the Prince of Wales Museum, is a diorama treasure trove. Further south, at the bottom of India, the Natural History Museum in Trivandrum is our favorite by far. On the other side of the taste scale are the anthropomorphic creations by amateurs, some of them inspired, some not. My college dorm room proudly sported three upright frogs in sombreros playing billiards, bought in Nuevo Laredo, Mexico, on a bender. Even less appealing is Rogue Taxidermy. Think of winged-monkeys, three-headed dogs, and other imaginary creatures straight out of nightmares. Some of the great collections are in obscure places like a funeral home in Madison, Wisconsin, which features hundreds of stuffed squirrels. The grandest purveyor of stuffed animals and the bits and pieces that go into them—glass eyes and plastic tongues, plus assorted crustaceans, insects, butterflies, and fossils—is Deyrolle, at 46 Rue du Bac, in Paris, an establishment in business since 1831. We prefer Claude Nature, at 32 Boulevard Saint-Germain, for a more boutique-like experience.

American taxidermist Carl Akeley had to slay this leopard with his bare hands by forcing his hand down its throat. Both man and beast look the worse for wear.

Hermes spent a weekend creating his own dioramas in our living room in Upstate New York. A close look reveals a crazy assemblage of the good, the bad, and the ugly, including rubber rats and freeze-dried frogs.

For more details about taxidermy, please visit: www.mgroupstuff.com/taxidermy

**OPPOSITE** I would never have thought I could pick him out of a crowd, as one penguin looks pretty much like another, right? But when I saw Jeffrey Rothstein's portrait of Andy Warhol I instantly thought, "That's our penguin." And it is. He stands almost two feet tall and has pride of place in our living room. Do we offer a charmed second life for these animals or simply a new hell on earth?

NAME: Slit gongs/Vanuatu
DATE: 1960s to 1970s

The islands that make up Vanuatu (formerly New Hebrides) have been populated for about 4,000 years. The first Europeans—Spaniards and Portuguese—stopped by in 1606. The next visit came in 1768. That little gap in the dance card speaks volumes. On a landmass the size of the state of Connecticut, over 120 languages are spoken, including pidgin, a French and English combination. It is a rough place, populated by tribes that practice cannibalism, battered by volcanic eruptions and typhoons, and very clearly off any beaten path. James Michener's 1947 Pulitzer Prize winning novel *Tales of the South Pacific* was set in Vanuatu, as was the Rogers and Hammerstein masterpiece, *South Pacific*.

Adam Johann Ritter von Krusenstern, the first Russian to circumnavigate the earth, published a record of his trip in 1815–1818 that included renderings of the exotic men of the South Seas.

An 18th century encounter between the Tanna people and the British navy was documented by William Hodges (1744-1787) in 1772–1775, when he accompanied Captain Cook on his second voyage to the South Seas.

In 1970, New York art dealer George W. Staempfli traveled to what was then the New Hebrides and negotiated the purchase of our *Atingting kon*, or slit gong from Tofor, chief of the Fanla. No small feat.

A postcard dating from around 1905 is of the men of Tanna, New Hebrides.

Our slit gong was carved from the trunk of a breadfruit tree in the 1960s and came to our house via the world-class tribal art collection of William A.M. Burden, Jr. He had parked it in the driveway of the family house in Hobe Sound, Florida. It has mates in the Michael C. Rockefeller Wing at the Metropolitan Museum of Art in New York and in the *Musée Quai Branly* in Paris. These drums are the largest standing musical instruments in the world, used for dance music and to send messages from island to island. The spiraling eyes represent the morning star. The curves by the arms are highly prized pig tusks, and the slit represents the mouth, and gives voice to the ancestor that the gong embodies.

The 14-foot-high slit gong at the Metropolitan Museum of Art is from Vanuatu and dates from the mid- to late-1960s.

For more details about oceanic art, please visit: www.mgroupstuff.com/oceanicart

OPPOSITE I was struck dumb the first time I walked into the room, and there stood our slit gong—huge, with those crazy eyes.

LEFT Over the bed, the large map of commercial airline routes after World War II was originally in the chairman of the Federal Aviation Agency's Washington office. It was a house-warming gift from his grandson, who knew Hermes loved maps and later gave it to him. All the routes and carriers are delineated, with little plastic tapes and named buttons. Who knew you could once fly directly from Santa Fe to Boise? The room is large and bright, so it could handle a rich brown paint by master colorist Donald Kaufman, and the big, bright Oushak carpet. It serves as Hermes' office in the country, with a fully extended cork-top dining table, by American designer Paul Frankl, that now functions as a perfect desk.

NAME: Maps and globes
DATE: Sixteenth century to today

Hermes is the map guy. Maybe it's that Cuban island mentality, as in "I've got to get off of this island," or the Cuban diaspora mentality, "Where to next?" Whatever the impetus, Hermes loves to travel and he loves maps. His collection spans from sixteenth century navigational maps, to nineteenth century Havana street maps, to twentieth century restaurant souvenir placemats. Maps satisfy on so many levels. Informative and beautiful, they document the expansion of our physical, scientific, and cultural worlds.

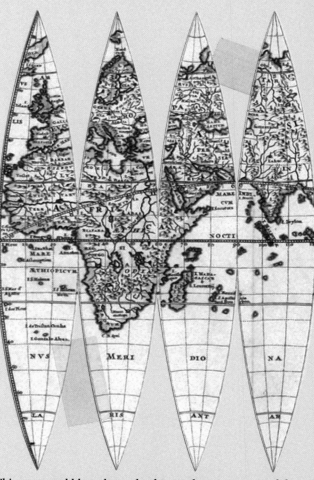

This gore would have been glued to a sphere to create a globe.

Hermes found this calligraphed Islamic map of the world in the Grand Bazaar in Istanbul, Turkey.

This three-dimensional plastic map is a souvenir of Cuba.

A 1930s map of Nouvelle Calédonie has a modernist play on the classic map cartouche, with natives displaying masks and produce. Hermes found it in a flea market in Paris.

The venerable Map Room at the New York Public Library, *above*, houses one of the world's greatest collections. For the Explorer's Ball, a fundraiser, Hermes and I decorated the corridor with illuminated globes and huge blowups, *below*.

A 1940s pictorial map of La Habana in beautiful pale blues and greens shows a city that has not changed much in 55 years.

Cartography took off in the fifteenth century with the Age of Exploration, the invention of the magnetic compass, and Gutenberg's printing press. By the seventeenth century, maps were being mass-produced. The great "Atlas Maior," an artistic and scientific masterpiece conceived by Willem Blaeu, was published in Holland in 1665 with 594 maps. It has been republished by Taschen in 2010 and is a bargain compared to the $1 million-plus an original would cost. Or you can see the real thing at the mother lode of maps—there are over half a million—in the Lionel Pincus and Princess Firyal Map Division of the New York Public Library.

A 1960s transistor radio doubles as a globe of the world.

For more details about cartography, please visit:
www.mgroupstuff.com/cartography

**OPPOSITE: Assorted maps and watercolors of costumes hang over an American Modernist table from the 1940s. The maps run the gamut from an eighteenth-century one of Havana, Cuba, to a 1950s school map of the United States.**

PRECEEDING PAGES
My little bedroom got spruced up with faux-bois wallpaper that truly fools the eye. The warm limed oak contrasts with the coolness of the blue wool curtains. The room opens onto a south-facing porch that serves as a study in the winter and a garden during the summer.

LEFT The bookcases, with their great, chunky rope handles, were made from former wooden armaments boxes.

OPPOSITE Kar-Mi was big in vaudeville around 1917, swallowing electric light bulbs, hypnotizing, reading minds, and shooting and then un-shooting his charming assistant, "The Great Leon." The chair is an English Gothic Revival piece. I bought it one Saturday at a Christie's auction, 20 years ago. Seeking instant gratification, I decided to try to put it in a taxi. Gil Perez, the best doorman in New York, and Christie's best human resource, held up his hand without much hope and what must have been the last Checker cab in New York rolled down Park Avenue and picked me and the big chair right up. I have never been in a Checker cab since. Remember the good old days, when we used to let other taxis go by as we waited for a Checker?

RIGHT The dining room is multifunctional, with a seating area, a big dining table, and two walls of floor-to-ceiling windows. The knotty pine ceiling and the Tibetan or Mongolian carpet drove the palette when we sought out Donald Kaufman's advice. He came up with a great, edgy pine green for the window trim that disappears in the day yet has enough yellow in it to be lively at night. Growing up in east Texas, in the shadow of the Big Thicket on the edge of the Piney Woods—the names speak volumes—we regarded pine trees as a crop, and the wood was junk for paper. But we moved back East, and instead of cutting them down, we plant pine trees and love them. It's all relative.

1 *Ceremonial Mask, West Africa, twentieth century.*

2 *Mahogany and cork and low table by Paul Frankl for Johnson Furniture Company, United States, 1950s.*

3 *Chair, United States, 1970s.*

4 *Majolica pottery tree-trunk garden stool, France, twentieth century.*

5 *Natural root wood mounted as a lamp, Japan, early twentieth century.*

6 *Carpet, Mongolia, late nineteenth century.*

7 *South Asian hardwood Elephant Chairs, carved from one piece of wood, unknown origin, early twentieth century.*

8 *Taxidermy ostrich hatchling, France, contemporary.*

9 *Wood carving of a toad with glass eyes, Japan, early twentieth century.*

10 *Pair of painted zinc window shutters, Paris, France, late nineteenth century.*

11 *American Empire gilt wood pier mirror, Albany, New York, 1840.*

12 *An early (pre-LV monogram) Louis Vuitton trunk, France, twentieth century.*

13 *Ceremonial porcupine quill fetish, New Guinea, twentieth century.*

14 *Rock crystal lamp by Mrs. Schneider, United States, 1950s.*

15 *Untitled #8, from the To Be or to Pretend, Roman Series by Adrian Fernandez, 2010.*

16 *Contemporary embroidered and overlaid cotton textile, India.*

LEFT A post-World War II oak sideboard by French designer Charles Dudoydt anchors a large 1954 canvas by American artist Bayard Osborn. The seventeenth century white marble Buddha head is Burmese, and the glass hurricane lanterns are made up of old and new bits.

OPPOSITE The bowed window does a whole ship's prow thing and is the right shape for a big round table. The now-faded textile on top of the wool tablecloth is from India. The Colima dog is a fake, but the Baga snake totem is real. The Elephant Chairs are carved from one piece of a hardwood Asian tree. The Mongolian rug is truly one of my favorite things. I have never seen such colors or wacky organic designs part-nered with bold geometric Chinese motifs—the butterflies, the big pods, the pomegranates, the totally Pop Art flowers. What were they smoking?

NAME: Aboriginal bark paintings
DATE: Pre-history to today

For over 35,000 years, Australia's natives have created art based on the stories of the Dreaming, the great oral history of the Australian people that has been passed on for millennia. This is the world's oldest continuous art tradition, and the framework for the spiritual lives of the Aborigines and their land.

Prehistoric rock paintings were found in Northern Australia.

In Central Australia, artist Bilinyarra Nabegeyo works on a bark painting in the late 1980s.

Bark paintings include one from the turn of the twentieth century, above left, and one that dates from about 1950.

Some of the motifs seen in 35,000-year-old rock paintings in Northern Australia continue to be used today, reflecting the incredible longevity of the Aboriginal experience. Aboriginal art is the last great art tradition to be discovered. It was not until the mid-twentieth century that native Australian art became globally appreciated. In 1967, Aboriginal political and social rights were legislated, and in 1971, Geoffrey Bardon, a white schoolteacher, introduced acrylic paints and paper to the Aboriginals. With this new, modern medium came an explosion of creativity and output. By the 1980s, museums and galleries were collecting and showing the art: an ancient and widely unknown tradition was suddenly being celebrated, and continues to flourish today. All Aboriginal art has a meaning. Behind every painting or object, there is a story connecting it to the earth and to the ancient culture's history: The art reflects what is held sacred and secret in the Aboriginal universe. Often, there is an almost aerial aspect to the work. *The Dreaming* and the landscape, for example, appear

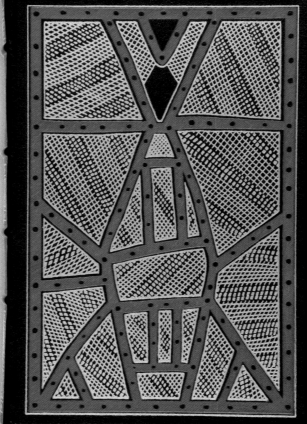

An Aboriginal design inspired the tooled leather cover of a first edition of *The Songlines* by English writer Bruce Chatwin.

An eighteenth century engraving illustrates two Aborigines defending their lands against the European colonists.

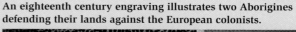

An acrylic dot painting by Tim Leura Japaljarri, an artist who worked in Central Australia, dates from 1975.

to be skeletal overviews. The paintings are created using materials found in the artists' immediate surroundings, such as fire-treated bark, white clay, and ochre pigments. Our collection is made up of ceremonial carvings and bark paintings, which we have mounted on large, leather-covered panels to allow for the uneven shapes of the eucalyptus stringbark.

📱 For more details about Aboriginal art, please visit: www.mgroupstuff.com/aboriginalart

OPPOSITE In the bar, one of a pair of mid-century Swedish chairs—very Flintstones—flanks the sofa. The low tables are covered in Chinese rice paper and may be stacked or staggered. They were originally sold at Bloomingdale's, in New York.

LEFT AND OPPOSITE
The bar was a mixed
blessing. From Day One
I thought it was pretty
great, huge, and funny.
Hermes, always the
voice of reason, was
not convinced. Then we
removed it—it's one
long piece of cabinetry—
to redo the floors, and
saw the room empty.
Long and narrow, the
space required the bar's
return. Fifteen years
later, we love it and
cannot imagine life
without it. Between
the Oceania pieces, the
Aboriginal art, some
African things, and the
wall of horns, it has a
Nairobi Hilton-on-the-
Hudson-River vibe. The
enormous mirror was
made by Geoffrey
Bennison for the fantas-
tic New York apartment
of Marie-Hélène and Guy
de Rothschild. It is part
Dutch seventeenth cen-
tury, part English 1980s.
The photographs are by
contemporary artist
Guido Orsini and the
carved wood angels are
from Goa, India.

OPPOSITE Across from the long bar, the book-cases are an homage to American designer Paul Frankl's famous Skyscraper furniture.

RIGHT I found these signs in Hudson, New York, soon after we bought the house. They were bright, graphic, very tall, and cheap. But what to do with them? One night, about 2 am, walking past them leaning on a wall, I had an inspiration: Mount one as the door to the powder room vestibule and hang the other next to it. Hermes was dubious, but they work.

# A close friend of ours decided to leave the non-neighborhood of Central Park South for Lower Fifth Avenue.

Her reasons were simple: She wanted outdoor space and she wanted to have her dog with her in New York—her previous co-op had a no-pets rule. Her apartment search was brief. One night, she had dinner with friends in their Fifth Avenue penthouse. Within a few weeks, they became her new next-door neighbors, and we began renovating the duplex. The apartment, which seems to have been carved out of the spaces for the water towers and building mechanicals, has a wonderful quirkiness, and tops a once-famous New York hotel where my grandmother had stayed when visiting my mother in the 1940s. It had long ago been turned into residences. Few of the window sizes or shapes matched each other, and only some of the rooms had four right angles. It is a tree house in Manhattan, and is as warm, welcoming, and fun as the person who lives in it.

There are three terraces, each facing a different direction, that provide both entertaining and private spaces. Off the bedroom, the terrace has windblown pines and ornamental grasses. On Day One, our client said she wanted an outdoor shower—"like the one I have in Palm Springs," she explained. Before wasting lots of valuable general contractor time figuring out the plumbing that would be required, I simply proposed that she take off all her clothes, go stand on the terrace, and then decide. Oddly, we never heard about the outdoor shower again.

The living room terrace has a wonderful wisteria-covered Romanesque brick façade. In the spring, you can smell the flowers before opening the front door. A sprawling roof space outside the kitchen includes a garden, with an apple tree, a barbeque, and a play space for her grandchildren. Happily, there was no need to cover the windows for privacy, just to protect from the sun, so electronic solar shades were all that were needed. There is also plenty of room for the canine, Zorro, who clocks in at four pounds.

The client's 25 years of living in France achieved what her Beverly Hills childhood and New York girls' school education had not: She cooks as if she learned to at La Tour d'Argent, the illustrious Paris restaurant, which she did. So the kitchen, with its three exposures of glass walls and a view north to the Empire State Building, is key. It is just large enough to work as an informal dining room, and so light and airy that everyone happily gravitates to it.

There were design challenges—low ceilings and a hodgepodge of window shapes and sizes. There was no order or symmetry, and too many expanses of blank walls. Nothing flowed; everything just stopped. The night the renovation was completed, as I sat alone contemplating the first floor in blessed silence after the chaos of bustling, semi-hysterical movers, cleaners, florists, and even decorators, I said to myself, "Carey Maloney, you are a #%*@ing genius!" I can't think of any other project that has given us as much satisfaction. Although our friend shifts from house to house and country to country, her true home has become this penthouse. Every space there truly works for her—and for Zorro.

OPPOSITE The terrace off the living room has spectacular open views to the southern tip of Manhattan. An arched, Romanesque-style wall is covered in wisteria. Although long and narrow, the space works equally well for large cocktail parties or for small dinners.

RIGHT The front hall does double duty as a dining room, the table extends to seat twelve. The rug is a Samarkand—where East meets West in multicultural Chinese and Persian motifs. Given the number of odd window shapes and sizes, we designed 'floating' lacquered bookshelves that allowed us to wrap the room and make the windows part of the design—happily making lemonade out of lemons.

1 *Attic black-figured pottery amphora, Greece, late nineteenth/early twentieth century copy of a 200 BCE vase.*

2 *Red lacquer tapered cabinet, China, nineteenth century.*

3 *Low table with inset Ming dynasty (1368-1644) stone panel, China, twentieth century.*

4 *Low chair by William Haines, United States, 1950s.*

5 *Cloud card table, cork top and mahogany legs, by Paul Frankl for Johnson Furniture Company, United States, 1950s.*

6 *"Plunging Neckline" side chair by Paul Frankl for Johnson Furniture Company, United States, 1950s.*

7 *Oscar, Academy of Motion Picture Arts and Sciences Award, Best Picture, Casablanca, 1943.*

8 *Carpet, antique Samarkand, Uzbekistan, late nineteenth century.*

9 *Renaud Contet, Bear, sculpture, France 1990s.*

10 *Renaud Contet, Bear, lithograph, France, 1990s.*

11 *Lamp in the form of a Chinese candlestick by William Haines, United States, 1940s.*

12 *Famille Rose figures with later-painted decoration, China, eighteenth century.*

13 *Anglo-Indian mahogany dining table, India, twentieth century.*

**NAME:** Milton Avery, 1885-1965
**DATE:** Twentieth century

Milton Avery was a great twentieth-century American modernist master whose refined and restrained paintings happily turn up often in our projects. His work—sort of figurative, sort of abstract, and always beautiful—is a key component in any American painting collection. The scenes are serene and easy, in the best sense of the word. "Everything I paint that isn't a cow is probably Sally," said Avery, referring to his wife, the painter Sally Avery.

A drypoint self-portrait of Avery that dates from 1937 is in the Smithsonian American Art Museum, in Washington, DC.

Avery painted pianist Annette Kaufman as her husband, violinist Louis Kaufman, serenaded them. Kaufman, due to his movie work, was the most-recorded musician of the twentieth century. Who knew?

Sally Avery and not one, but two cows, grace this canvas in a house we designed in Connecticut.

A blue ox? Is it Babe of Paul Bunyon fame or just a random blue ox in this Avery painting, *opposite*.

The first Avery we worked with was a big, approximately 50-inch square, post-1945 abstract oil painting. The clients were very serious about their art and they wanted the walls and the carpeting to be a color they described as "mouse"—a grey-taupe neutral color that would work with everything they had. The collection included pieces of African primitive art, numerous boxes by American artist Joseph Cornell, and Viennese furniture. We agonized, as that kind of color can suck the life out of a room if it isn't done right. After much deliberation, we achieved the perfect "mouse" hue and painted every wall with it. That is, it was perfect until the Avery arrived to be hung and we saw that about one quarter of the canvas matched our mouse color exactly: It was a complete Milton Avery camouflage.

Shown in a photograph from around 1950, the dining room in a Wallace K. Harrison-designed house in Northeast Harbor, Maine, includes an Avery painting of the Maine coastline. Isamu Noguchi carved the table on site, and the curved glass walls were made by an aeronautical windshield manufacturer.

After much gnashing of teeth (mine), the painting was removed and given to the National Gallery in Washington, D.C., on loan, where it remains to this day. A friend of ours once found an Avery rolled up in a coat closet after her mother had died. Her father had never liked it, so it had languished there for thirty years. It's not hidden away anymore. And it depicts an ox. I wonder if that beats a cow, value-wise? Another one of our clients commissioned Avery in the 1940s to paint a view of "their" Maine coast. If one faced the wall across their dining table, which they had Japanese sculptor Isamu Noguchi carve on site, one could see two Avery oils of the ocean view behind one, reflecting the view like a mirror. Incredible. The record price at auction for an Avery is $2,500,000. Recent auction prices have ranged from $50,000 to $1,400,000.

**Milton Avery**
**& THE END OF MODERNISM**

This catalog accompanied the 2011 exhibition at the Nassau County Museum of Art, in Roslyn Harbor, New York.

For more details about Milton Avery, please visit: www.mgroupstuff.com/miltonavery

**OPPOSITE** The landscape by Milton Avery hangs over a custom-made George Nakashima mantel shelf.

**NAME:** Trophies/Oscars/Awards
**DATE:** Nineteenth and twentieth centuries

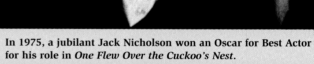

As far as accessories go, awards and trophies are fun. As they are personal and unabashedly self-aggrandizing, I try to avoid placing them front and center on the living room mantel, where the winner is constantly reminded of past triumphs. Speaking as someone with no trophies, and at the risk of sounding embittered, I think it's key that they be placed with care and discretion. When in doubt, the powder room qualifies as very discrete. The Nobel Peace Prize is the apex. A Heisman turns heads in football circles. And of course, there is the Academy Award, or Oscar, the ultimate herald of success in the movie business.

The 1851 *Emperor's Plate*, made by R. & S. Garrard & Company, the famous silversmiths in London, was a gift from Czar Nicholas of Russia as a trophy for an Ascot horse race. Visible among the many motifs of heraldry and dragons, a sled is being chased across the steppes by wolves, as the driver fends them off with a whip, and the passenger uses his pistol. The trophy fetched $890,000 at auction.

A cache of family yachting and racing trophies fill a mantel under a portrait by Thomas Sully, of a funny looking, but very important, ancestor.

A twentieth-century silver trophy with stag-horn handles has sadly lost its original inscriptions, which are often removed to make way for new winners.

In 1975, a jubilant Jack Nicholson won an Oscar for Best Actor for his role in *One Flew Over the Cuckoo's Nest*.

According to a 1939 World's Fair press release, eighteen-year-old Leonard Centrone won a trophy for being the Handsomest Iceman in New York.

Obviously, there are Oscars and then there are OSCARS. Our client inherited her father's statuettes—two for Best Picture for two of the indisputably greatest films of all time. The little nine-pound statuettes are gold-plated representations of an Art Deco-style Crusader, his sword resting on five reels of film. The statues have no intrinsic value, but the few that have been sold have brought in serious money. In 1999, Michael Jackson paid $1,542,500 for David O. Selznick's Best Picture award for *Gone with the Wind*. Only pre-1950 Oscars have any market value, as post-1950 winners have to contractually give the Academy of Motion Picture Arts first refusal for $1. When these iconic accessories have come up for sale, some flush past winners have paid up to buy them and then return them to the academy in an effort to maintain the mystique. It's fine to recycle other people's winnings. We found three huge wicker trunks filled with tarnished yachting and racing trophies in a client's barn. I leapt on them with glee while the 20-somethings scratched their heads. After some serious polishing, the footed-and-handled urns became a family treasure, documenting their sporting past.

For more details about trophies, please visit: www.mgroupstuff.com/trophies

**OPPOSITE** An Academy Award, or Oscar, is displayed by one of the windows in the company of a penguin by American artist Tom Sachs.

LEFT The kitchen has three exposures, with a view north to the Empire State Building. Vintage cement Moroccan tiles and a lot of sun warm up the glass aerie. There is an espaliered apple tree on the brick wall outside. The photograph by the sink is by Mexican artist Lourdes Grobet, from her series on Lucha libre, her country's over-the-top professional wrestlers.

**NAME:** George Nakashima, 1905-1990
**DATE:** Mid-twentieth century

Before George Nakashima, the great furniture makers forced wood into submission, creating perfectly book-ended veneers and inlays and using rare woods as a medium, like paint or tiles in mosaics. Nakashima used the tree, knots and all, to create his iconic, free-form twentieth-century furniture. We came to Nakashima when I wanted something Malibu-casual for a New York bedroom. We thought about a driftwood mantel, which were in short supply, so I thought, wouldn't a vintage Nakashima mantel be cool? Calls to dealers were made, but those vintage mantels were in even shorter supply. "Have Mira make you one," was the advice I was given. We took it.

The barrel-vaulted poolhouse at the New Hope, Pennsylvania, compound was built in 1960 and furnished with Nakashima furniture and straw *tatami* mats.

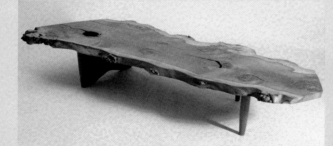

The woodworker's design fodder was burls, knots, and imperfections. "Trees have a yearning to live again," he said.

A pilgrimage to the Nakashima Studios in New Hope, Pennsylvania, was required, where we selected our own pieces of wood from the vast barns and sheds, and met Mira, George's daughter and heir to his design firm. The compound is amazing—each building is a mid-twentieth century gem. The finishing studio floor is layered with decades of spilled linseed oil, creating an incomparably rich black natural linoleum surface that I immediately coveted. Nakashima came to his furniture design after a classic American education at the Massachusetts Institute of Technology, a European grand tour, time spent working for architects Frank Lloyd Wright and Antonin Raymond in Japan and India, and his internment during World War II. Upon the family's release, they moved to New Hope and began their firm. New York governor Nelson Rockefeller was Nakashima's grand patron: In 1973, he commissioned over 200 pieces of furniture for his Japanese house in Pocantico Hills, in Tarrytown, New York. In Manhattan,

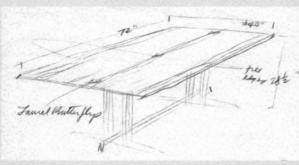

A sketch shows a Frenchman's Cove Table, which was first designed in 1967 for a Jamaican resort, and is still in production today.

The walnut Minguren I End Table 1 is quintessential Nakashima, and pure sculpture.

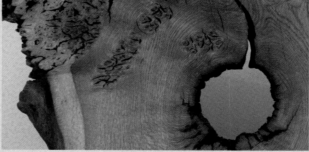

Nakashima worked with the entire tree and honored its oddities of knots and imperfections.

Nakashima's work can be seen in the Cathedral of St. John the Divine, where he installed his Altar for Peace in 1987, and in the Metropolitan Museum of Art, where a room is devoted to his work at the culmination of their Japanese collections. One of our best friends grew up in a 1950s house in New Jersey that was full of Nakashima. The first thing out of my mouth was, "What did the neighbors think?" The last laugh is theirs, though, as the prices for custom-made pieces by Nakashima, as well as for the mass-produced, now vintage, pieces that he created for the Knoll and Widdicomb furniture companies, have gone through the roof. It all makes sense. His work is absolutely wonderful.

In 1945, George Nakashima was photographed with his precocious woodworking child, Mira. She grew up designing furniture, and today, runs the company.

The elegant Mira Chair is available in three heights, for children of all ages.

For more details about George Nakashima, please visit: www.mgroupstuff.com/georgenakashima

**OPPOSITE** I don't really like cats, but I love this crazy earthenware art nouveau cat by French artist Emile Gallé, who sits on a stack of nineteenth-century quill- and tortoise-shell boxes in the master bedroom. The headboard is by Mira Nakashima, whose father was the famed furniture craftsman, George Nakashima.

# It was a happy day when this couple called us. They were very smart, very attractive, and very excited about designing a new apartment. Young, too!

It's more fun shopping in Paris with pretty and glamorous people rather than with old and cranky ones—we've done it both ways.

They bought a grand, very grown-up duplex in Manhattan in August, hired us, and it was gutted to its retaining walls by Labor Day. That's when the fancy Park Avenue "summer-only" buildings stop all construction until around the following Memorial Day. So when May finally arrived, lots of people leapt (fifty to sixty men a day worked on the two floors), and three months later it was all built, with everything new, but looking as if it dated to the late 1920s. The building board's collective jaw dropped. Two months later it was decorated and turned out to be, as far as we were concerned, a wonderful project.

This is one of the ones that we could move right into. The 1929 building is a Park Avenue gem by legendary architect Rosario Candela, with an incredibly chic lobby designed by the legendary Dorothy Draper—all black-and-white marble, a fountain—which I love—and Duncan Phyfe-style furniture. Our narrative was to create the apartment the building owner might have put together, himself, in 1929. We chose restrained Art Deco details and made everything on a grand vertical scale, which we then painted with the flattest of paints so that bronze-and-nickel staircase would glow in front of the matte background. Adding the ancient Greek white-marble stella worked well for us, too, as did the glossy-brown tortoise lacquer walls and the snow-white rug in the dining room. The Greek and Egyptian white stone pieces float in front of glossy ethereal surfaces.

We had access to the family's vast and varied eye-popping collections. When we went to one of their homes to "shop," seeing there would not be a dearth of materials, we had free rein to pitch the idea of, for example, all-Roman bronze body parts in the powder room, or perhaps a couple of dozen Mayan stone masks in the guest room. We found piles of Pre-Columbian textiles, shelves lined with Mayan and Incan sculpture, a pack of Colima dogs, and a herd of magnificent Tang horses. We chose Art Nouveau glass from the greatest Tiffany patterns. Our generous guide, the family patriarch, knew about each and every object in incredible depth. It was amazing—the best pieces in the world, with no sordid money issues, and an excellent return/exchange policy!

OPPOSITE The esplanade between the lanes of Park Avenue traffic is a wonderful urban amenity. A block association sees that the flower beds are beautifully planted. Every spring there is a new tulip color. The flat steel sculpture that looks three-dimensional is by Venezuelan-American artist Rafael Barrios. It is part of a series of nine of his pieces that were exhibited on Park Avenue in the Spring of 2012.

**NAME:** Greek sculpture/marbles
**DATE:** 510 BCE to 323 BCE

For 150 years, from 510 BCE until Alexander the Great's death in 323 BCE, Greece and its capital, Athens, created the foundations of our Western civilization. During this classical period, philosophy, medicine, science, theatre and, of course, the fine arts, all flourished. The pure white marble sculptures of ancient Greece epitomize the period, and the work of sculptor Praxiteles was its apex. His figures of gods were perfect, idealized specimens, and the gods he chose to sculpt were the young ones—Apollo, Hermes, Aphrodite—and not scruffy old Zeus. In his hands, polished white stone became translucent flesh and the poses he achieved were not just life-like but represented real movement and emotion.

A servant offers her mistress a coffer of jewels in the fifth century BCE, *Stele of Hegeso*, a funerary memorial.

His Aphrodite of Cnidus was the first life-sized female nude. The model for the goddess was supposedly Athens' most prized courtesan, Phryne—and everyone who was anyone had seen her naked. The natural poses achieved are called *contrapposto*, or "opposite pose," with the figure standing with most of its weight on one foot, forcing the shoulders and arms to twist off-axis from the hips and legs. A few of our clients have collected Greek, Roman, Etruscan, and Egyptian antiquities. The great Greek marbles are the most fragile and rare, as Greece was small, the classical period was short, and marble breaks easily. The big pieces are the *stelae*, which were used as standing monuments or place markers, sometimes funereal, sometimes geographic. Carved in deep relief, they memorialized the wealthy and powerful, and offer valuable insights into Greek home life BCE. Visit the Acropolis in Athens to get an idea of the work in situ. Then check out expat marbles, such as the Elgin Marbles in the British Museum in London, or the Pergamon Altar at the Pergamon Museum in Berlin for the mother lode. All neat, clean, and safe in European capitals, pending the chronic litigation for repatriation by the locals who lost them. Turkey collected 15 million signatures when it attempted to grab back the Zeus altar in 1991, but the Germans resisted and the altar remains a German national treasure.

This fragment of a frieze came from the Parthenon, a temple to the goddess Athena, on the Acropolis in Athens, Greece.

We have lots of vintage photographs of Praxiteles' marble sculpture of Hermes, our favorite Greek god.

The *Aphrodite of Cnidus* by Praxiteles, from the fourth century BCE, is also called the *modest Venus*. This ancient copy, in the Glyptothek Museum in Munich, Germany, lost her arm, or you would be able to see her hand covering her nakedness.

📱 For more details about Greek sculpture, please visit: www.mgroupstuff.com/greeksculpture

**OPPOSITE** The lovely woman in the Greek marble stele at the foot of the staircase in the hall is so serene and patient she looks like she could be waiting for a cross-town bus in heaven. Hermes designed the lyrical bronze stair-railing with monel accents—a combination of nickeled silver and copper—to reinforce the luxurious, yet abstracted, neo-classical theme we created for the apartment. M (Group) designed the macassar ebony sculpture base.

NAME: Georgia O'Keeffe, 1887-1986
DATE: Twentieth century

Georgia O'Keeffe is an indisputable American icon. Not only does her work have great strength and force, she looks physically tough and purely American. Her New Mexico desert subjects are painted with precision, but abstracted. She got up close and personal with a flower, and created botanicals for a modern age. Realism was modern through her eyes. She gained recognition in New York in 1916 at an early age and was a successful female artist, which was rare at the time. She moved from New York to the desert around Santa Fe, New Mexico, in 1949, where again she was a woman in a man's world—windblown and sunburned in her cowboy boots and leather skirts.

O'Keeffe was married to art dealer and photographer Alfred Stieglitz, who took this portrait of her in 1918. Stieglitz showed her work in New York at his avant-garde gallery, 291, along with a stable of artists that included painters John Marin and Arthur Dove, and photographer Edward Steichen.

New Mexico's art community was a very small world in the 1940s. O'Keeffe's friend, American master photographer Ansel Adams, took this photograph in 1942 of an adobe church in Taos Pueblo that is now a UNESCO World Heritage Site.

"I have but one desire as a painter—that is to paint what I see, as I see it, in my own way, without regard for the desires or taste of the professional dealer or the professional collector," she said. Perhaps this attitude explains why, when she died at the age of 99 in 1986, she owned half of her more than two thousand known works. You have to admire her independence. We love her art. From the moment I saw one of our client's incredible landscapes from her *Pelvis Series*, I complained bitterly about the frame. Sure, it was original. But it was so small, so cheap looking, and it did nothing for the painting. I figured it was all she could get out there in the boonies of New Mexico. It was removed and carefully returned to storage, and a new, white lacquer frame was designed. As it turns out, O'Keeffe was consumed with her frames. What I thought was an afterthought was actually an extension of her artwork. Her framer, a New Yorker named George Of, worked very hard on her simple silver-gilded clam shells. By the 1950s, her exhausted framers developed and patented the clamshell metal-section frames that allowed us all to cheaply frame our posters, and became rich in the process. We live and learn, and learn, and learn.

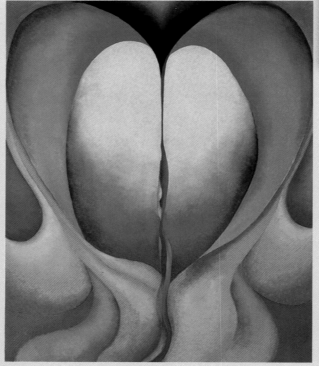

Considering the art produced in the United States immediately after World War I, the 1919 *Series 1, No. 8* is wildly ahead of its time. The sensuous forms and the vivid palette raised eyebrows in New York's art world.

A view of Ghost Ranch, O'Keeffe's home in Santa Fe, New Mexico, for over forty years, is seen through the sitting room to the garden.

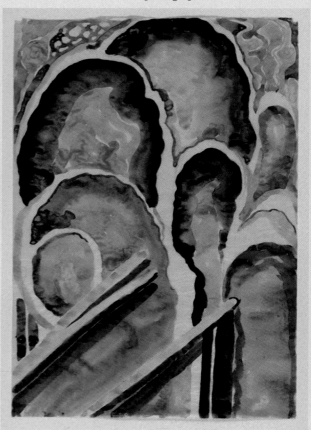

The *1916 Blue #1* watercolor and graphite on paper is now at the Brooklyn Museum in Brooklyn, New York.

For more details about Georgia O'Keeffe, please visit: www.mgroupstuff.com/georgiaokeeffe

OPPOSITE Across from the staircase in the front hall are tall pairs of doors that lead to the library, and living and dining rooms. The hall is painted in a creamy flat white, with recessed panels and shallow reveals. The Chinese altar table under the O'Keeffe painting is Ming dynasty. The Roman bronze head fragment and the African Dogon figure are treasures.

RIGHT The living room is a favorite of ours. It's cool. The furniture and objects are very fine and the scale is sort of grand, but it's still cool, stylish, and relaxed. The room was laid out to function in the twenty-first century: A big television set becomes the family hearth, and guarantees the room is used. A pale beige flat paint with almost white trim keeps it fresh. The enormous Sultanabad carpet has a fantastic dark turquoise blue in it.

1  *Pre-Columbian terracotta seated figure, Mexico, 500 to 1000 CE.*

2  *Louis XVI marble mantelpiece, France, late eighteenth century.*

3  *Art Deco side table, parchment top, United States, 1930s.*

4  *Standing lamp by Bagues, Paris, France, 1940s.*

5  *Pair of macassar ebony veneer folding screens by Jean-Michel Frank, France, 1930.*

6  *Pair of Art Deco bergères, France, around 1930.*

7  *Pair of Lucite and pony skin ottomans, Vladimir Kagan, United States, contemporary.*

8  *Pair of side chairs, Harvey Probber, United States, 1950s.*

9  *Bronze horse, Rome, first century BCE.*

10  *Carpet, Ziegler Sultanabad, Persia, late nineteenth century.*

11  *Pair of terracotta figures of ladies in waiting, China, Tang dynasty, 618 to 907 CE.*

12  *Pair of wood, metal, and leather military "treasure trunks," China, nineteenth century.*

13  *Gilded and painted six-panel "sudari" (bamboo roll-up shade) pattern screen, Japan, nineteenth century.*

14  *Marble sculpture, Cyclades Islands, Greece, 3300 to 2000 BCE.*

OPPOSITE Three floor-to-ceiling windows face the avenue and are covered in a pale cashmere shade and double-faced silk chenille curtains.

RIGHT The Richard Serra hung over the Louis XVI black-and-white marble fireplace confirms yet again how well black and white works against natural wood. A carved wood African stool serves as a coffee table near the French Art Deco club chairs, which still have their original leather and came from a flea market in Paris.

## NAME: Oushak rugs/Turkey
## DATE: Nineteenth and twentieth centuries

We are rug nuts. Oushaks are probably our favorite carpets. They aren't the most expensive carpets, and they can be casual or formal, and are available in large sizes. Some are just expanses of a beautiful faded color with shadowy patterns, and others, with their large scale patterns, are wildly vivid. One reason we gravitate to Oushaks is their loose, large weave—a double-knot method, as opposed to Persian rugs, which are woven with a tighter single knot. We find the less-fine manufacture to be a good foil for extremely fine rooms.

Textiles and rugs are draped across the divan, cover the floor, and festoon the interior of a harem, as depicted in this 1877 canvas by French painter Fernand Cormon.

We also love a beautiful bare wood or stone floor of course, and we've done lots of successful rooms without great rugs. But more than once I've thought, "Let's try a fancy rug in here," and immediately the room comes together and feels completed. The rugs of the Turkish city of Oushak have been prized for centuries. Cardinal Thomas Wolsey, 1473-1530, ordered 60 Turkish rugs in 1520 via the Venetian doge for Hampton Court Palace. It must have been nice—Henry VIII moved in after the cardinal fell from favor. The industry waned as the taste for Oushaks in Europe changed and carpets woven in the West became available. It was only in the late nineteenth century that the Oushaks experienced a renaissance. The later pieces, woven using tribal techniques with palettes of reds, ochers, pale greys, and blues are the rugs we see today. The rugs once covered the floors of the great mosques in Istanbul, with sometimes three or four laid atop each other. The valuable old rugs were replaced with machine-made copies as the originals were sent to Western markets. We have used a lot of Oushaks and have also owned quite a few. Auctions are a great way to obtain one—"Does it fit the room?" and "Does it fight the room?" are important questions to ask. We've gotten excellent bargains. Unsure about the size or colors? Our advice is to find a polite, patient rug dealer of good repute, shop, and arrange to try out a few in the room. Don't be shy about looking at lots of rugs—the guys unrolling and rolling them have more stamina than you think. With me, it seems as if the last one I see is the one that I end up buying. I had an angora Oushak for a while. The wool was so luxurious it seemed to glow. It was very cool, but in the long run, too glowing. The Anatolian wool is naturally lustrous, so beware of chemically washed rugs that really shine. The same applies to tulus, the long-haired nomadic weavings. If the color isn't found in nature, it shouldn't be in the textile. We've bought Oushaks for $2,000 and for $200,000. The vast range pretty much sums up the prices of rugs in general. Condition, aesthetic, size, provenance, and age all add up, sometimes to $2000, and other times to $200,000.

A Turkish rug was featured in *The Ambassadors*, 1533, by German master Hans Holbein the Younger. In the sixteenth century, the carpets, known as Holbein rugs, were very valuable pieces used to cover tables or beds rather than floors.

A pale Oushak carpet dating from about 1890 was originally woven for the European market.

The Angora goat is a fragile animal and does not travel well. The first herd sent to the United States in 1849 as a gift from the Ottoman Sultan Abdulmecid did not survive. The rugs made from Angora mohair have a lustrous, opulent sheen.

In the Grand Bazaar in Istanbul, rug dealing is depicted in an old photograph as a low-stress, hookah-smoking profession.

📱 For more details about Turkish Oushaks, please visit: www.mgroupstuff.com/oushakrugs

OPPOSITE The bright Oushak rug in the library was chosen at the beginning of the design process as the clients understood the importance of committing to a rug early in the game. The Art Deco furniture, including the game table, the chairs and the desk, are all by French master Jacques-Emile Ruhlmann. They are so refined we used matte wool flannel for the curtains and cashmere window shades to act as a foil to the glossy wood and dazzling rug. The rectangular hammered-iron curtain hardware adds a note of ruggedness to the room.

NAME: Roman sculpture/portrait bronzes
DATE: 1 CE to 330 CE

Roman art is accused of being Greek art's poor and vulgar cousin. Indeed, the Romans copied the great Greek works by the thousands, and without these copies, many ancient Greek pieces would have been lost forever. But Rome was a different cultural and political animal than little Athens. The vast empire was always absorbing new cultures and provinces, and the vast population was materialistic to a fault. There was a frenzy of acquisition of objects, including Greek art, as booty from different wars.

An 1896 illustration of the Roman army is from a collection of 32,000 prints and images of military uniforms donated to The New York Public Library by Samuel J. Tilden in 1911.

The Romans valued family above all else. Portrait busts from the Republican era threw aside idealized beauty and opted for brutal realism. Granny was out there, warts and all, because she was grand, and a Roman's relatives and ancestors defined his social position. Far from being ashamed of the wear and tear on an old face, Romans looked to facial features as a sign of wisdom, experience, and nobility. Often busts, a Roman innovation, were used for the family shrines found in every upper class home. If there was a famous consul or senator in the family tree, portraitists tried to imbue the current subject with the same recognizable features. Social and political climbers would steal ancestors in order to add to their own allure and status—a bronze bust predated DNA tests. The bronzes were political statements and traveled to the four corners of the

The first century CE statue is of a young noble Roman of the Julio-Claudian clan. His eyes would have been made of ivory.

Fig leaves were slapped on the masterpieces of ancient art by modern churches and museums. London's Victoria and Albert Museum kept a spare, with hooks for portability, in case the chaste Queen Victoria stopped in.

empire. Portraits in public places celebrated military and political achievements. When the tides changed, the bronzes of the out-of-favor leaders were melted down.

Mercury, or Hermes in Ancient Greece, the god of merchandise, taking a break on a boulder, is the official god of *Stuff*.

A fragment of a portrait bust of Emperor Marcus Aurelius dates from 121 to 180 CE.

For more details about Roman sculpture, please visit: www.mgroupstuff.com/romansculpture

OPPOSITE A Roman head stands on a pedestal in the living room, which was kept pale and matte. The adjacent richly glazed and glossy dining room has tortoise-shell-colored walls with gold dust floating in the paint surface. Rug dealer Doris Leslie Blau described the antique Kashan rug as looking like snow. It is wonderfully lustrous and feels clean and fresh. The wool for these rugs was sent to Persia from mills in Manchester, England.

## NAME: Ivory furniture and objects
## DATE: Seventeenth to twentieth century

There are few subjects less politically correct than ivory furniture and decorations. Who would still promote further depleting the dwindling elephant population for their tusks? Not us. We've cooed and swooned the few times we've been close to an elephant. Ivory can come from elephants, hippopotami, whales, or walruses. It has been prized for thousands of years. The Greeks and Romans loved it, and its popularity in classical times resulted in the extinction of North African elephants. History seems to repeat itself. But the things we've dealt in are very, very old. What's done is done.

The sixteenth century ivory *Queen Mother Pendant Mask, Iyoba,* from the Edo people of Nigeria, is a masterpiece of African art.

Ivory hunters showed off prized tusks in Dar es Salaam, Tanganyika, around 1890.

A detail of an 1860 Napoleon III-era carved Dieppe mirror frame shows a coronet and monograms flanked by putti playing flutes. 'DB' is presumed to be the Duchesse de Berry, a patroness of Dieppe.

Angayarkanni, the elephant of the Meenakshi Sundareswarar temple in Madurai, India, blessed me. I needed it after padding around those filthy floors in my bare feet.

And ivory is a treasure for a reason. It is beautiful. From the Renaissance to the nineteenth century, the port of Dieppe in the north of France was a center for the carving of African ivory. As the valuable cargo trickled, and later flowed, in, it was first carved into religious imagery. As tastes and times changed, the ivory was used decoratively.

This late-seventeenth century Dieppe-ivory pocket sundial with penwork decoration was made by Charles Blood.

The original carvers were sailors who honed their talents on the long voyages home, and then established workshops in Dieppe. I would not advise buying ivory abroad, or tortoise shell, or anything made from endangered species. Even a tiny ivory knob on a little box can cause you big problems at customs.

The eighteenth century ivory-veneer side chairs, from Vizagapatam, India, are based on a 1762 design by Thomas Chippendale, the English furniture craftsman. They are from Kentshire in New York.

For more details about ivory, please visit:
www.mgroupstuff.com/ivory

OPPOSITE In the dining room, a Dieppe ivory mirror has been hung above one of a pair of consoles designed by M (Group). The console top doubles as a dining table extension. The Greek bust is a consummate example of Classical purity, and we think the mirror, an example of nineteenth-century excess, is a good contrast.

NAME: West African sculpture
DATE: 1,000 CE to 1930 CE

Africa is a huge continent with a vast array of cultures and religions, from the Berbers in North Africa to the Zulus in the South. Beginning in the fourteenth century, both Islam, which was expanding to the south of the Sahara Desert, and Europe, which was on the brink of the Age of Exploration, were interested in Africa for the raw materials they could extract, and the human beings they could convert or kidnap. There was little interest in the arts or cultures of the African peoples, as they were dismissed as primitives. Early in the twentieth century, the artistic climate was ripe for the discovery of African art.

The Mende women are a cultural rarity in Africa, as they have their own secret societies, ceremonies, dances, and masks.

Antelope headpieces, by the Bambara people of Mali, were pivotal in the development of twentieth century European art.

Terracotta Nok figures from 500 BCE to 200 CE are the oldest-known figurative sculptures south of the Sahara, and were discovered only in the middle of the twentieth century.

Paul Guillaume, a destitute Parisian automobile mechanic, found some African carvings in a shipment of rubber tires. He displayed these pieces and captured people's attention—this is how African art was introduced to the avant-garde artists of the day, including Pablo Picasso, Amedeo Modigliani, Marie Laurencin, and Georges Braque. Guillaume became a leading art dealer and his *Sculptures Nègres* exhibition in 1917 was the first show of its kind. The timing of Guillaume's lucky find was perfect. Modern artists were obsessed with abstraction, cubism, and the reorganization of forms, and the "new" African art was elegant and reductive, imbued with mystical and religious meaning. The stylized *Chiwara* antelopes from Mali were among the first African sculptures to grab the attention of the European intelligentsia and, coincidentally, my first piece of African art was a *Chiwara* headdress made by the Bambara tribe in the central African nation. I bought the 30-inch-tall wood carving in Cape Town, South Africa, for $120, after much gnashing of teeth, as I was 21 years old at the time, and on a student's travel allowance, and I would be traveling for thousands more miles carrying this awkward, fragile thing. But I had to have it. And after three months of angst, I got it back to my dorm room. Bambara

A Bambara (Mali) hunter rendered by a French artist late in the 19th century.

antelopes are used in agricultural fertility rites, and always dance in male and female pairs. The figures are tied to a straw headpiece, and the dancer is shrouded in long, dangling grasses that represent rain. The Dogon and Senoufo people of Mali resisted Islam, both the religion and its enslavers, and moved deep into the hills and mountains to protect their culture. The tribes produced the *ne plus ultra* of the African art world, the iconic seated figures of men and women. With bodies reduced to cylinders, breasts to cones, and eyes to diamonds, the best of these pieces exude a primordial power that few naturalistic western figures can match. These figures are intensely private objects and were hidden in caves when not in ceremonial use. Some are thought to be over 800 years old. A Senoufo piece, the Burden Rhythm Pounder, set the auction record for African art when it was sold for $1,250,000 in 1995.

For more details about African art, please visit:
www.mgroupstuff.com/africanart

**OPPOSITE** There is a cross-cultural theme to the vignette in the living room. An antique Japanese screen hangs above an eighteenth century Chinese military treasure-trunk chest, which has been used as a side table. The African terracotta head on the right is from the Nok tribe and dates from between 1000 BCE to 500 CE. The 1940s rock-crystal lamp is one of a pair by a lady named Mrs. Schneider. I don't know anything else about her, except that we love her lamps.

LEFT Powder rooms allow for a freedom of expression. They're always tiny and should make guests smile. An American Art Deco cupboard was converted into a vanity, and the space is lighted by a pair of Tiffany Studios Chain Mail sconces.

RIGHT The vanity in her bathroom is made of sycamore, with parchment-wrapped doors. The sconces are by American designer Tommi Parzinger, with glass balls hanging independently of the fixtures. The onyx wall tile is slightly translucent.

**NAME:** Eugène Printz, 1889–1948
**DATE:** France, 1920s to 1940s

Of all the great masters of French Art Deco furniture and decoration, we worship at the altar of Eugène Printz. If Jacques-Emile Ruhlmann is considered *le roi* of French Art Deco, for us, Printz is *le grand dauphin*. Printz's choice of materials was inspired. Rough-hewn Gabon ebony or figured palmwood was juxtaposed with designer Jean Dunand's ultra-refined lacquer. Gilded and hammered iron was looped and curved to create supports that defy gravity.

Printz was photographed by Laure Albin-Guillot wearing eye-glasses that would be favored by twenty-first century architects.

A monumental sculpture mural of the flora, fauna, and peoples of the world covers the façade of the 1931 building that is now the Palais de la Porte Dorée, on avenue Daumesnil in Paris.

The salon du Maréchal Lyautey in Paris is still intact—a miracle, considering the incarnations the Palais des colonies building has experienced since 1931.

His designs, with his version of primitivism, are much more to our taste than the reflectively polished *ébène de Macassar* that other makers favored for their overly refined work. Printz's work is never precious, but it is dear. Prices for large pieces can easily exceed $1 million. His designs for the fantastic *salon ovale du Maréchal Lyautey* in the *Musée des Colonies* at the *Exposition Coloniale Internationale de Paris* in 1931 set the benchmark for Art Deco elegance, as far as we are concerned. Rare woods, hammered metals, and primitive motifs were used to create rooms that celebrated France's colonial triumphs. The marshall's reception room, the *Salon d'Asie*, had an Asian theme with murals by André-Hubert and Ivanna Lemaître of the world's great religions, including a meditating Buddha, an opining Confucius, and a cavorting Krishna. Over 33 million people visited the exposition to see its pavilions devoted to the peoples and cultures of the world, including a "human zoo." Given the clueless nature of the zoo, it is not surprising that this was the last gasp of the European colonial masters. The museum building is one of the great examples of the 1930s Paris School of Modernism, with a huge bas-relief by Adolphe Janniot spanning

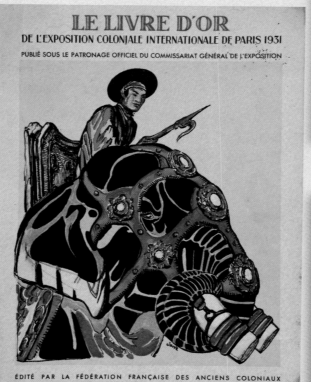

The catalog for the 1931 Colonial Exposition in Paris is full of images of the pavilions and gardens built to represent the far-flung colonies of France.

A masterpiece Printz sideboard with lacquer panels by Jean Dunand comes from the Gallerie Vallois in Paris.

the front, which is covered in colonial imagery and happily toiling natives. The building is now the *Cité Nationale de l'Histoire de l'Immigration*, and the Printz room remains intact. Make the pilgrimage to see it and the adjacent masterpiece, the *Salon d'Afrique* by Jacques-Emile Ruhlmann.

*Printz* by Guy Bujon and Jean-Jacques Dutko is the definitive book on the designer. It was published by Les Editions du Regard in 1986. The cover is a beauty—that red is fantastic.

For more details about Eugene Printz, please visit: www.mgroupstuff.com/eugeneprintz

**OPPOSITE** This bedroom has a small Printz sideboard in rosewood, with gilded bronze *sabots*, or feet. The standing lamp is from Tiffany Studios, and the elegant parchment, bronze, and glass bench is by an unknown designer.

**NAME:** Tiffany Studios
**DATE:** United States, 1885 to 1910

The beautiful leaded-glass shades of Tiffany lamps have been victims of their own popularity. They were quickly, and poorly, copied in the late-nineteenth and early-twentieth centuries, and the name became eponymous with the brand. The real ones are rare. The great ones are hen's teeth.

The Peacock pattern, *top*, shows the variety and complexity of the glass used in the best lamps; a Lotus table lamp dates from about 1904, *center*; and the Wisteria pattern, *above*, is deservedly one of the most famous designs. The vine base supports a carpet of flowers.

**The recently restored Veterans' Room in Manhattan's Seventh Regiment Armory is one of the great extant Tiffany Studios-designed rooms.**

Louis Comfort Tiffany, 1848-1933, was an heir to Tiffany & Company. He began his career as a painter, then segued into interior design, eventually expanding his work to glass—and later to enamel, jewelry, mosaics, and silver. Tiffany Studios received plum commissions, like Chester Arthur's White House and Mark Twain's Hartford house. His own 580-acre place on Long Island Sound, Laurelton Hall, clocked in at 84 rooms. Tiffany did well for himself. His glass pieces are amazing technical and artistic achievements. The great patterns incorporate huge varieties of glass—dense and opaque pieces, thin transparent bits, confetti glass with tiny flecks of color—in shapes and thicknesses that achieved painterly effects. The bases and bronze mounts are equally complex, and the combinations are fantastic. By 1905, there were over 120 patterns, with names like Nasturtium, Geranium, Bamboo, Dragonfly, and Magnolia. The "Chain Mail" pattern, with lead-framed glass squares inspired by medieval armor, is one of my personal favorites. Less exuberant than the floral designs, the pattern creates a warm, diffuse light and can work in contemporary rooms. Tiffany lamps have a bad reputation in the design world. When was the last time anyone saw one in a home design magazine? One problem is that serious collectors tend to put multiples in a room, which is always a killer: Too much of any good thing is a bad thing. Another reason the lamps aren't seen very often might be explained by how expensive they are. The auction record for a Tiffany lamp was $2.8 million, set in 1997.

Louis Comfort Tiffany as a young interior designer, around the time he decorated the Chester Arthur White House.

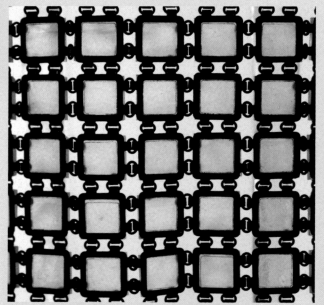

**The Chain Mail pattern is one of our favorites. I've used sconces and hanging fixtures, and covet the fire screens, but none of our clients has indulged me to date.**

For more details about Tiffany Studios, please visit: www.mgroupstuff.com/tiffanystudios

**OPPOSITE In the guest room, a yellow Laburnum-pattern Tiffany Studios lamp sits on a Wiener Werkstätte table, flanked by French Art Deco chairs. The stool is African.**

LEFT The kitchen succeeds in breaching two seemingly disparate design goals—hygiene and coziness. The white crackled tile that lines all the walls and sheaths the pantry doors, the enameled-steel light boxes and the stove hood, as well as the white-marble countertops, all say "pristine." The cream palette keeps the space soft and friendly. Instead of art, we opted for a huge framed stone fossil and a nineteenth century French clock, both easy to wipe down.

# I always say there is nothing better than a party to ensure a deadline will be met.

Clients who had bought Treetops, a grand old house in Westchester County, New York, in August, announced they would be having a little house-warming in November. They had hired Robert Isabell, the world's best and most expensive party planner, and the date was written in stone. We knew the guests would be A-List, so the gauntlet had been thrown down. "What a great idea!" I muttered weakly. What I was really thinking—"Are you nuts?"—was impolitic.

We have a two-out-of-three rule: fast and/or cheap and/or good. In this case, since fast and good were givens, cheap went out the window. We rallied our forces and promised a finished product—including landscaping, the exterior, and the interiors—in three months. The lady of the house wanted a new, state-of-the-art kitchen—though she didn't cook—and the man of the house had a bee in his bonnet about a knotty-pine library. We were doing the normal soup-to-nuts scope, but with only moments to design and build. One concession was for all of the upholstery—both furniture and curtains—to be in muslin. It would be a good backdrop for Isabell's party extravaganza, and meant there would be no compromises due to tardy fabric shipments. Water gilding the curtain rods was to stay in the schedule. The only real glitch was finishing the library. Knotty pine is a dicey soft, cheap wood that needs slow and careful staining, and some nasty chemicals, to force a patinated, even glow. When done right, it is magic. Doing it wrong was not an option, so we had a nice man flown in from North Carolina two days before the party to polish it up.

All was finished on the Friday night at 11 p.m. for the next day's festivities. Fights with testy party planners were almost forgotten as the tents and acres of flowers were installed. It was all pretty fantastic. We drove back to town exhausted, but with visions of our glorious return the next night dancing in our heads. On Saturday morning my phone rang. A call at exactly 7 a.m. is never good news. My blood ran cold. The call began, "No one was hurt but..." Okaaay... keep going.... It turned out there had been a fire the night before. Wood-staining rags—that damn pine—had combusted in the basement, sending smoke throughout the house. The fire was small, but the smoke was huge. Chaos had ensued as women and children were evacuated in the snow to a friend's house. Six fire engines screamed up the drive, knocking over the party lighting. We raced back to Westchester. Fire clean-up people were summoned and did what they could, given the timing. Isabell brought in dozens of bottles of his secret smoke eliminator. We lit every fireplace in the house—there were maybe ten—to give the illusion that the smell of smoke was natural. At 7:30 p.m., we got dressed in the basement and stumbled to the bar, shell-shocked. All in all, it was a smashing success. And it made for great cocktail conversation. "It is pretty, isn't it? You wouldn't *believe* my day." At dinner we had *primo placement*, which reassured us. We had survived the fire and the clients were still our friends.

OPPOSITE The original Colonial Revival house, known as Treetops, had been expanded over the years. Most of the original woodwork was removed. Hermes added the quoins at the corners, as well as panels, shutters, and a pergola. The house colors are stone greys and blues, which feel very Westchester, New York.

OVERLEAF The wisteria-wrapped porch off the living room becomes an outdoor living space in the summer. Classical columns support the balustrade of a roof terrace, which can be accessed from the second-floor bedrooms. The outdoor furniture is new, but has a 1940s look reminiscent of Maison Jansen, the Paris firm.

## SALVAGE

**NAME:** Architectural elements
**DATE:** Eighteenth to twentieth century

Not everything in a room should be grand and perfect. Sometimes the volume needs to be taken down a bit. It keeps one humble. We have wandered through many a salvage yard in our day. The valuable lesson we have learned is to let the dealers forage in the filthy graveyards and wait for the treasure after it's been culled—old gasoline-station signs, tin ceilings, bronze elevator gates, exit signs—we've used them all. The word salvage comes from the Latin *salvus*, to save. Originally a nautical term for post-shipwreck clean-up, it has broadened to include saving and recycling almost anything.

The five panels from the *S.S. Normandie* are only a small part of the ship's 4,300-square-foot mural, *The History of Navigation*.

A seventeenth century carved sandstone-and-wood Mughal façade was taken from an Indian palace to be sold in the West.

The most glamourous twentieth-century salvage might be the 1935 verre églomisé panels from the *S.S. Normandie's* dining-room mural, *The History of Navigation*, by Jean Dupas. The Art Deco oceanliner sank in New York harbor in 1942 under suspicious circumstances, and the salvage effort was the most expensive in history. There can be issues around salvaged stuff. Retrofitting is easier said than done. Weight must also be factored in. The 1920s bronze elevator gates are seductively elegant but they are scarily heavy, so modern versions are perhaps more functional—I learned that the hard way. A capital on a stone column will make a handsome low table, but will the condominium floor support its weight? The demolition of Pennsylvania Station, New York's great Beaux Arts masterpiece, designed by McKim, Meade and White and completed in 1910, began in 1963. The great eagles were salvaged, and some of the huge marble columns were later found in a New Jersey dump. The silver lining in this tragedy was the resulting creation of New York City's Landmarks Preservation Law in 1965.

Fifty years after its demolition, Pennsylvania Station remains the poster child of urban renewal gone awry.

*Night*, a work by American sculptor Adolph Alexander Weinman, dates from around 1910. The figure holds a bouquet of drooping poppies and once framed a massive clock in the magnificent Beaux Arts Pennsylvania Station in New York.

A pair of ornate bronze grotesques are early twentieth century electrical-switch–plate covers.

For more details about salvage, please visit:
www.mgroupstuff.com/salvage

**OPPOSITE** We used carved-wood corbels from a building cornice for the console table in the airy front hall that is open to both the front and the back of the house. The corbels needed attention, as bits and pieces were filled in, and the paint required touching up. We like imperfect things that we can tweak to make them functional, but still leave them heavily distressed.

RIGHT Knotty pine is a favorite wood of ours. This wood is cheap but the finishing process is key. This wood was oxidized and then French polished; it is warm and welcoming, and looks like it has always been there (in a good way…). The pine paneling is very American but the decoration has elements from far afield. The black-and-white Robert Mapplethorpe photograph snaps against a wood background.

1 *Louis XV fruitwood fauteuil, France, eighteenth century.*

2 *African antelope skin and raffia wrapped drum, contemporary.*

3 *Regency brass dolphins mounted as lamps, England, around 1820.*

4 *Pair of bronze "rain" drums, Thailand, twentieth century.*

5 *Robert Mapplethorpe,* Flower, *1980s.*

6 *American Empire side table with a slate top, New York, nineteenth century.*

LEFT The wall of glass that separates the plant-filled sunroom from the dining room can be opened up for big dinner parties. Furniture is kept to a minimum. A French Empire chair is paired with an old hourglass that we bought in Hudson, New York, which now functions as a side table.

RIGHT The living room is big and has three walls of arched windows. There is tons of light, and wonderful views of the gardens. The late Robert Isabell, the great party planner and flower genius, put together the huge bouquet of delphinium. The upholstered furniture is as simple as it gets, and the pieces of antique fruitwood furniture share a classical spirit. The big, beautifully detailed, and water-gilded bamboo curtain rods are favorites of mine.

**NAME:** Treehouses

**DATE:** Seventeenth to twenty-first century

It must be primordial or something, but I like to be off the ground. For safety? A good sightline? Perhaps a nice nesting place? From the time I was very young, I retreated into the Texas trees. When I was MIA to get on the nursery school bus, people always knew to simply look up. All I ever wanted growing up was "a parrot, a monkey, and a treehouse." While the monkey was nixed, I did get Eric, a meat-eating mynah bird, and I jerry-rigged my own treehouse.

The Maple of Ratibor (Italy) was a two-story living garden folly. The topiary could easily hold forty guests.

The isolated tree-dwelling Kombai and Korowai tribes of Papua New Guinea live eighty feet above ground. These lofty perches help them elude their cannibal neighbors.

Collectible nineteenth century cigarette cards were included in packs of smokes, and covered subjects from sports to bathing beauties and geography, like this Kombai treehouse. The priciest card sold in 2007 for $2,800,000.

This little jewel at Pitchford Hall in Shropshire, England, claims to be the oldest treehouse in Europe.

After renovating the main house at Treetops, outside of New York City, and building a new guesthouse, we all agreed that the next phase would include a treehouse for the kids. I was thrilled, and saw it as a fringe benefit of a career that has been the vicarious fulfillment of my childhood fantasies. The large property boasted a veritable arboretum, so we had a lot of good contenders for our planned two-story house. We decided to use the trunk of a massive, but storm-damaged, tree as our foundation and immediately called in structural engineers. When in doubt—and to best avoid sleepless nights—pass your treehouse plans by an expert first. We wanted stairs, not ladders, and we had to have multiple levels. We gave it a pirate vibe with ropes and nautical motifs, and furnished the treehouse with lots of wacky

bits and pieces from our basement, all painted the same shiny dark brown. An obligatory picnic basket was fastened to a rope and pulley so that it could be raised and lowered for provisions. The oldest known treehouse is the English Elizabethan-style Pitchford Hall aerie, which is all plaster and half-timbered, and at least 300 years old. The tree itself clocks in at 900 years old. Queen Victoria visited it as a young teenager. In contemporary times, the epicenter of the treehouse movement seems to be the Pacific Northwest, where there are plenty of trees and plenty of hippies. There are some great books on the subject, with sample plans and good advice, written by charming architect and builder tree-hugging types.

For more details about treehouses, please visit: www.mgroupstuff.com/treehouse

**OPPOSITE The treehouse on the property, our design gift to the whole family, was the realization of one of my childhood dreams. It's fun, and for all ages—from little pirates and princesses to teenagers texting "Treehouse. Now."**

# When we first renovated our clients' main house in Katonah, New York, Hermes and I thought: "This is plenty big. They are rich in family space. What more could anyone need?"

But when the number of children went from three to seven, new construction—and a space for the parents and their guests to retreat to, in particular—became necessary. Hermes designed the guest house to reflect the area's equestrian vibe, using large, arched horse-stable doorways. The building was designed to be exactly 10 square feet in plan and one foot shy of the maximum height allowed without public review, in order to avoid any discussion by the busybody wannabes on the town review board. The clients had lived through Hermes' vivid and horrible reports from previous Manhattan and Westchester boards, and they were eager to avoid that process. Good design needs some parameters and givens. In this case, the given was Hermes' sanity.

The property is large, and the guesthouse is completely out of sight of the main house, adjacent to a spectacular tennis court that is carved into the hillside. With its own entrance and driveway, it is certainly private. There are two large bedrooms, two extra-large bathrooms, a big, high-ceilinged living room, and a media space above the billiard room, which is connected with a simple, handsome, curved staircase. The mix of furniture is definitively high–low, with lots of Hudson, New York, finds and hand-me-downs from the clients' other houses. It all comes together as being fun, comfortable, and user-friendly—exactly what a good guest house should be.

OPPOSITE The porte-cochère acts as access to the main courtyard of the house and tennis court, which is located 50 yards to its right. As it is left open for a large part of the year, it also serves as an interior hallway to the second bedroom and the steam and sauna rooms. We happen to love interior-exterior spaces. They are not just reserved for sunny Western climes, but can work on the East Coast, too.

RIGHT The Living Room ceiling and woodwork are roughhewn wood, with exposed beams and structural elements. The main house could err on the side of "grand," so the guesthouse aesthetic is a bit more raw. The room reads as monochromatic but is actually painted in four similar pale-khaki colors. The black-and-white David Hockney print of an odalisque pops against the red brick of the fireplace.

1 *Gothick-style brass lamp, England, 1920s.*

2 *David Hockney, lithograph.*

3 *Art Deco leather club chairs, France, 1930s.*

4 *Low table, formerly a bed with rattan top, China, early twentieth century.*

5 *Carved wood ceremonial shield, Sepik Valley, Papua New Guinea, twentieth century.*

6 *Pair of tall, tapered red lacquer cabinets, China, nineteenth century.*

7 *Louis XV fruitwood fauteuils, France, mid-eighteenth century.*

# NAME: Tulas/Suzanis/Ikats
# DATE: Nineteenth and twentieth centuries

Turkish textiles used to be rare, but now with our design globalization, things we seldom saw before are ubiquitous. Take suzanis for example. These large embroidered pieces are used as bed covers, room dividers, baby wraps, or horse blankets. Practically at birth, Uzbek women start working on their wedding dowries. By the time the big day rolls around, the average middle-class girl has ten suzanis in her hope chest. Our first trip to Istanbul turned into a frenzy of textile shopping. Once we had seen the handsome and typical black and red embroidery, we wanted the softer and rarer colors. After we discovered suzanis, we segued to tulus—smaller, usually 3- by 5-foot woven pieces with long angora hair.

A detail of a *suzani* shows its exquisitely executed silk needlework on a linen field.

Sultan Suleiman the Magnificent (1494-1566) expanded the powers of the Ottomans far beyond Constantinople, threatening Europe's capitals, and sowing the seeds for centuries of conflict between Islam and the West.

Around 1872, a Jewish spinner, wearing a bright *ikat* coat, twists silk to make thread for fine weavings in Tashkent, a major trading city on the Silk Road.

I love this mid-twentieth century Angora *tula* weaving from central Anatolia for its Marin County hippie vibe. The wool—long, shiny, and very important, since *tulas* were used as blankets—is cozy and warm.

A nineteenth century photograph of a robe vendor shows his incredible selection of *ikat* menswear. The equally vivid linings are often quilted cotton in floral patterns or stripes.

Avoid the hot chemical-looking colors and seek out earthier tones, and whatever you do, keep them away from the cat. We bought four tulas, and a few weeks later, in Paris, we saw one hanging with pride of place over a Louis XVI lemonwood console at the super-chic Galerie Camoin-Demachy on the Quai Voltaire. Validation—decades of therapy later, and I still crave it. We segued to the silk ikats. For us, the suzanis and the tulas worked well for covering a bed or decorating a sofa. But ikats, woven on

narrow looms, are smaller and too fragile to just throw around, and are thus more of a collectible—as we usually focus on the functional. We ended up with a few beautiful ikat coats as parting gifts from a dealer. Those last-minute gestures of lagniappe, of which we get our fair share, confirm we paid too much. Even at my most delusional, I know it wasn't about my charm. For the ultimate in the genre, see the catalog from the 2005-2006 "Style and Status: Imperial Costumes from Ottoman Turkey" show from the Arthur M. Sackler Gallery at the Smithsonian Institution in Washington, D.C.

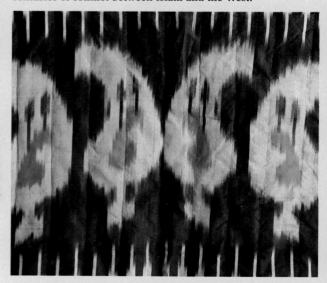

The process of creating vibrant silk *ikats* is extremely complex —involving a combination of dyeing and weaving techniques that go completely over my head.

For more details about Turkish textiles, please visit: www.mgroupstuff.com/turkishtextiles

**OPPOSITE** The headboard in the second bedroom is an old, banged-up section of a tin ceiling that was found in Hudson, New York, covered in generations of paint—just what the room needed. A suzani is used as a bedcover.

# We are worker bees. The luxury of living in a grand Manhattan apartment in a primo location will always elude us. So we make do, and we do pretty well.

Hermes' apartment, for example, is a floor-through in a townhouse on the Upper West Side. The block is famous for its allée of plane trees. The light is dappled and the view is charming. The size and scale of the proper and nearly square rooms work well for an architect. Since the living room is a working study, where Hermes writes and does research, we took the Chinese scholar's route and had him surrounded by inspiration: The desk is a Chinese table flanked by Anglo-Indian cabinets that house a television, as well as stacks of red-linen boxes filled with reference materials. Hermes is not into a typical home-office look, so we concealed everything related to his writing in interesting leather and lacquer boxes, Venetian paper folios, and Qing dynasty bowls for holding paperclips and laptop accessories. The Korean screen creates a vista into an imaginary world, and Hermes' rocks, pencil cups, and various containers were each chosen to inspire him.

The bedroom is lined with plaster casts and sculptures and has an ultimate Murphy bed, which is always tucked away to free up floor space. You have to love a bed that makes itself. The plaster cast collection began in the early 1990s with a nice old man on Lexington Avenue and 68th Street who was retiring his casting business. We bought one or two a month from him. Then we found our majestic Agrippina at Vincent Mulford's shop in Hudson, New York. That was the point when we segued into the larger-than-life and free-standing figures.

Front-to-back townhouse living can be rough. A room lined with books and a kitchen link the bedroom to the living room. The arrangement works by ignoring the function of the kitchen completely: Hermes had the gas disconnected, and uses the oven for storage. Some of his hundreds of vintage photographs disguise the cabinets. Hermes spreads out upstate. In town, he focuses.

OPPOSITE The residential side streets on Manhattan's Upper West Side, with their brownstone and limestone row houses, connect two of New York's most important parks, Central Park and Riverside Park.

RIGHT In the living room, the wall of windows faces north. That may not be the best light—a southern exposure would be better—but there is plenty of glass to let it all in. The pale Ghiordes carpet helps lighten the space, and a palette of light brown grasscloth mixed with warm brick-reds and mossy greens was chosen to bring the outside in. A happy potted palm always works for me.

1 *Pair of standing lamps made from seventeenth-century Italian carved-wood candlesticks, Italy, twentieth century.*

2 *American Empire piano stool, United States, circa 1820.*

3 *Victorian tufted sofa, England, circa 1860.*

4 *Plaster cast of Eros, United States, twentieth century.*

5 *Red-and-black lacquer table, Gracie Inc., New York, twentieth century.*

6 *Steer-horn stool, United States, early twentieth century.*

7 *Carved wood heddle pulley, Yoruba people, West Africa, twentieth century.*

8 *Mahogany game table with brass mounts, Germany, circa 1790.*

9 *Aboriginal bark painting, Unknown artist, Australia, circa 1980.*

10 *Louis XIII large armchair, France, seventeenth century.*

11 *African beaded headdress, Yoruba people, West Africa, contemporary.*

12 *Carpet, Oushak, Turkey, early twentieth century.*

13 *Suzani textile, Turkey, early twentieth century.*

NAME: Scholar's rocks

DATE: Sixteenth to twentieth century

We had a client who had a great Tang horse. It was of incredible rarity and huge value—a big handsome stallion, glazed in apple green. This particular client focused his collecting on French Art Deco furniture and Asian art, and each thing in his apartment was a treasure. So when we turned a corner on our first visit and spotted this two-foot-tall glossy black rock that made a ping sound when he flicked it, we knew it must be very important. But what was it? It turned out to be a Ming dynasty, 1368–1644, *ling bishi gong shi*, which translates as "spirit rock" or "scholar rock," an object of contemplation and inspiration. We were instantly enamored.

In the eleventh century, Emperor Huizong destroyed bridges to allow his barges to carry enormous rocks to the imperial gardens, and in the process, decimated the economy.

A nineteenth century painting of Lu Gong, the eighth century scholar, depicts him working in his garden with a huge blue rock outcropping looming over his table.

This fifteenth century *lingbi* scholar's rock is from Eastern China.

The staggeringly dramatic Huangshan mountain range in eastern China is a UNESCO World Heritage Site, and has been a subject for Chinese artists for centuries.

From desk-ornament size to gigantic garden versions, *gong shi* are prized in China for the beauty and grace of their natural shapes. Who knows what has been manipulated? Have they been carved, or worn away by hand? Cynically, I assume they all have. Regardless, the gravity-defying bases and the stances of the rocks certainly inspire reflection: "How the hell does it do that?" I am partial to the small ones that recall mountain ranges or billowing clouds of grey stone smoke on very decorated and highly polished wood bases. These rocks, along with ink pots, brush rests, and other Chinese writing implements, have been prized for centuries by the literati, and today still command big prices.

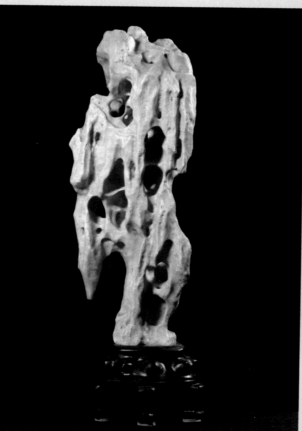

A large, ghostly white rock, probably from Lake Taihu, in eastern China.

A *lingbi* scholar's rock seems to effortlessly span its rosewood base, carved with a rock motif.

For more details about scholar's rocks, please visit: www.mgroupstuff.com/scholarsrocks

**OPPOSITE** Stone beads from the annual Quartzite Rock Show in Arizona fill a jadeite bowl that has been placed next to a small Chinese scholar's rock in the living room.

PRECEEDING PAGES Hermes spends a lot of time at home at his desk, so we found a large Chinese table to serve as his primary work surface. A pair of nineteenth century teak Anglo-Indian cabinets conceal the television set and dozens of storage boxes filled with research materials. The painting gives him a view of an eighteenth century Korean garden—a window into a fantasy world, which we grabbed at a client's estate sale.

LEFT Agrippina—we just call her that—came from the art department at Vassar College via Hudson, New York. Her custom-made base is also a storage cabinet—there's no such thing as unused space in Manhattan. A Peruvian manta has been thrown over the back of a Louis XVI-style chair. I kept telling myself "They are so packable!" as we bought about thirty of these hand-woven textiles in Cuzco, Peru. The contemporary painting with an African tribal motif was a gift from a client.

OPPOSITE Our heroic soldier was a total fluke of a purchase. He was one of maybe five lots of Chinese Revolutionary art in a summer auction at Sotheby's. I left a ridiculously low bid—and we got it. He is a treasure. The mirror is an eighteenth-century Swedish giltwood piece.

NAME: Revolutionary artifacts
DATE: 1949 to today

China has four thousand years of dynastic history, from the Xia Dynasty in 2000 BCE to today's People's Republic of China, with its Communist Party chairman Mao Zedong as the last great emperor and despot. For his new China, Mao dictated that art be for the masses: Art should educate, illuminate, elevate and, of course, further the cause of a socialist China. The varied and cheap media were posters, wood blocks, and pamphlets used to spread the government's message across the world's most populous nation.

Chinese Socialist realism was meant to be *hong guang liang*, or red bright shining—as conveyed by this mass-produced porcelain figurine that is literally uplifting.

The Cultural Revolution of the 1960s saw a surge in poster and printmaking as in this 1964 *Learn from the People's Liberation Army and thoroughly implement revolution* image.

Mao Zedong waves cheerfully on the 2008 book published by the Asia Society and Yale University Press.

The small ceramics made during this time are collectable and decorative. Lithe dancers and smiling youths predominate, but sometimes the subjects are 'way grim and too vivid, so we stick with the cheerful ones. Thirty years after the Cultural Revolution, the art has become mainstreamed via major museum and gallery shows in the West. China's new artists are vocally at the forefront of a movement toward greater freedoms. Communist or not, the new Chinese elite are spending big bucks, with China's art market now second only to that in the United States.

I bought this paper cut-out for pennies in Canton in 1979, the year the United States and the People's Republic of China normalized relations.

The revolutionary style was Socialist Realism, and the art was created to be *hong guang liang*—red, bright, shining. For this art, Hermes and I try to put the politics aside, which is easier said than done, but we love the stuff for its heroic quality. Our larger-than-life painted plaster bust of a soldier certainly qualifies—that kid exudes Hero. To say Mao's image was ubiquitous is an understatement: Over 2.2 billion items were made in the 1960s with his portrait. The chairman's image was crocheted on fabric panels that must have provided many a Chinese house with a room divider. Hermes continues this tradition and mounted his to disguise a door.

In Quartzsite, Arizona, I discovered a source for Chinese wares from a mineral dealer who travels annually to China.

What better vehicle could there be than postage stamps to spread revolutionary fervor? Joseph Stalin and Mao Zedong shake hands on this 1950 Chinese stamp.

For more details about Chinese revolutionary art, please visit: www.mgroupstuff.com/revolutionaryart

OPPOSITE A large, bright-green Awaji-ware vase sits on an eighteenth-century Chinese stand by the front door. The Japanese pottery is typically green or bright yellow, and a few of the pieces we have—one of which I happily found under my grandmother's kitchen sink—are wrapped with raffia. We found the rough cotton-and-wool panel of a young Mao at a rock show in the Arizona desert. Go figure.

LEFT The sandstone
sculpture is from a
temple in Northern India,
where it was once part of
an ensemble of gods.

RIGHT A carved African heddle pulley, originally used for weaving, stands on an eighteenth-century German folding game table. The model of a Braniff jet airplane might have once sat on a travel agent's desk. The Aboriginal bark dot painting includes snake and crocodile imagery.

**NAME:** Plaster casts

**DATE:** Nineteenth and twentieth centuries

For hundreds of years, the world's greatest sculptures have been seen and enjoyed far from their European originals. Plaster copies, cast directly from the sculptures, have allowed artists to study the masterpieces full-scale. The finest marbles and bronzes from antiquity have been copied and migrated around the world. To make them, the original piece is covered in wet plaster, which creates a negative impression. The empty form is then filled with plaster. The big ones, like our Hermes of Praxiteles, would be made from a couple of different casts, as they are large and very heavy.

My grandfather, Arthur Maloney, and the sculptor, Gaetano Federici, were photographed in 1935 in the artist's New Jersey studio. The plaster sculpture was a full-sized maquette that would be cast in bronze.

A 1903 stereograph depicts the Greek marble figures in the Acropolis Museum in Athens, from which plaster casts were made.

London's Crystal Palace Art Union, around 1861, housed a huge collection of plaster casts made from Greek marbles.

The first famous collection was assembled by Leone Leoni, a sculptor and a buddy of Michelangelo, who began collecting copies of the most celebrated sculptures in the world for his Milanese palace. The best casts are the first-generation casts made from the original marbles or bronzes. Often, they ended up surviving the originals to become our only connection to a masterpiece of the past. As generations of casts are made, the surface details are lost. America's greatest collection was at the Metropolitan Museum of Art in New York. Thousands of architectural elements and sculptures from antiquity to the eighteenth century were on exhibit in the great halls in the late-nineteenth century, before the young museum could afford the treasures it would later be able to purchase. The casts were on view for decades, but by the 1950s, the collection was dispersed to various universities or put into storage.

Federici made this plaster-relief portrait of my father, Edward Maloney, when he was four years old, in 1929.

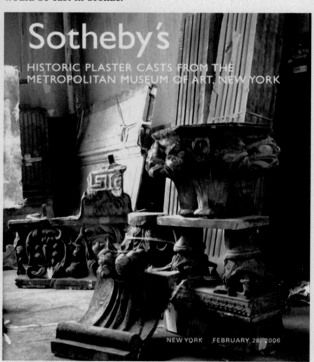

In 2006, Sotheby's auctioned some of its historic plaster-cast collection from the Metropolitan Museum of Art in New York.

📱 For more details about plaster casts, please visit: www.mgroupstuff.com/plastercasts

**OPPOSITE** Hermes' collection of plaster casts has grown, and his available wall space has shrunk. The casts come from a variety of sources, including shops, flea markets, and cast manufacturers. The best are old and were the models for casts, leaving a wonderfully colored patina.

NAME: T.H. Robsjohn-Gibbings, 1905-1976
DATE: Mid-twentieth century

Scottish-born designer T.H. Robsjohn-Gibbings made waves in the United States with his classical view of design. His 1944 bestseller, *Good-bye, Mr. Chippendale*, instructed the post-World War II American public to forgo antiques for a new, modern style. His great strength was his obsession with the motifs of the past, which informed his Modernist designs. His whopper commission was the Casa Encantada in Bel Air, California, a classical Greco-Georgian mansion built between 1934 and 1939, for which he designed over 200 pieces of custom-made furniture.

Robsjohn-Gibbings surveys an appropriately classical scene while lounging on one of his daybeds in Greece in 1961.

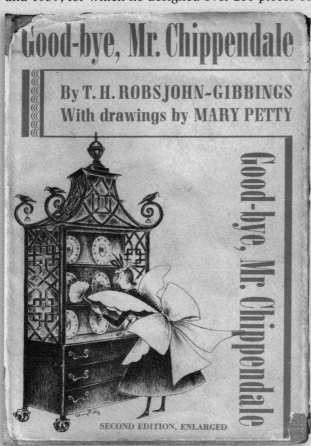

The furniture designer became a media star in post-World War II America with his best-selling book, which slammed the design establishment.

A game table and chairs by Robsjohn-Gibbings mixes well with Biedermeier and mid-century pieces in a living room designed by M (Group).

The elegant "Klismos" chair from Robsjohn-Gibbings' collaboration with Saradis Furniture in Greece in the 1960's remains in production.

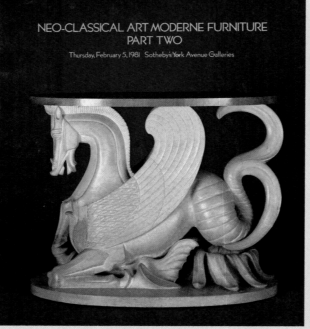

The catalog for the 1981 Sotheby's auction put the collection on the map—and on the block. We bought our cabinets and cherish the catalog with its low prices scribbled in. Hindsight!

The house and its contents were sold intact to Conrad Hilton, of hotel fame, in 1950. After Hilton's death in 1979, it was sold and the contents were auctioned by Sotheby's in 1981. The estate hasn't lost any of its gloss, and remains one of the most valuable houses in the United States today. The pair of bedside cabinets that are now in Hermes' New York apartment are from that Sotheby's auction. Blond wood with acanthus motifs, they are quintessential Robsjohn-Gibbings designs and must have come from one of the most luxurious of the fifteen bedrooms in Casa Encantada. A bronze swan covers the electronic controls for the radio and the bells to summon the staff. The other half of the pair features a tiny drop down desk concealed behind the top drawer. As one of America's foremost designers, he brought his taste to the masses by creating very successful furniture lines for Widdicomb Furniture Company and Baker Furniture Company.

The radio cover with its swan handle and acanthus border is a super-luxurious touch.

For more details about T.H. Robsjohn-Gibbings, please visit: www.mgroupstuff.com/robsjohngibbings

OPPOSITE In the bedroom, one of the pair of Robsjohn-Gibbings' cabinets sports a flip-down desktop instead of a drawer. The other half has a built-in radio with a bronze neo-classical swan. The cabinet, with its pale wood, acanthus-leaf ornamentation, and tiny swags for handles, is quintessential Hollywood Regency.

LEFT Casts of gods and George Washington are features of the fireplace wall in the bedroom. The cabinets are from the Casa Encantada in Bel Air, California, which was decorated by T.H. Robsjohn-Gibbings between 1934 and 1938. The fireplace is original to the house. We had the paint stripped and waxed to make it look like a plaster panel. President Washington was found in the trash outside a public school on Manhattan's 57th Street and Second Avenue in August. He was heavy and it was very hot, but I managed to grapple him five blocks and drop him off with a friend's doorman.

**NAME:** Adivasi terracotta

**DATE:** Nineteeth and twentieth centuries

I have whined my way around the world—"I don't need to see another church, temple, or UNESCO site—I *need* to shop." I maintain that I get to know the local people and traditions best through commercial interactions. During a trip, as we drove around southern India, every hole-in-the-road village had an enormous statue of a loco-looking dude with a major mustache, huge teeth, and crazed eyes, sitting on a horse, at the entrance. Then, seeking huge bronze pots in Kerala, India, we were pointed to an old lady's garden. There were no pots, but I took a peek behind the bamboo hedge and there, in the dirt, was a row of big terracotta figures—elephants and horses, complete, or in bits and pieces. Those big statues were hidden treasure. I was vindicated, yet again!

A herd of Ayyanar horses guard a village in Tamil Nadu, South India, in a 1970s photograph.

Hermes was photographed at the moment of discovery in Cochin, Kerala, on the Southwest Indian coast.

We began the process of negotiation, which for me boils down to, "I'll take it. I wonder how we'll get it home? How much is it?" This drives Hermes crazy. He reminds me gently that I am supposed to get a price *before* I say that I'll take it. We already had a container in the process of being filled, so, in a way, shipping was free. It was a very educational purchase. India's indigenous tribal population is about 60 million strong, and there are tribes all over the country. In the south, for thousands of years, the spiritual leaders were usually the potters who sculpted the guardian, the god Ayyanar, with that mad grin, sitting on his usually painted-white horse or between his two Technicolor wives. These Tamil Nadu village guards, sometimes 18 feet tall, are the largest hollow terracotta sculptures on earth. Terracotta is a South Indian alternative to stone.

The Sivalingam, representing the Hindu god Shiva, the Auspicious One, and his male energy, is flanked by equally energetic looking guardians in the Sri Meenakshi temple in the southern Indian temple town of Madurai.

The god Ayyanar, shown uncharacteristically with a shy smile and no handlebar mustache, is flanked by two consorts in this illustration. Ayyanar spends his nights fighting evil gods and assorted demons. So do I.

The famous Hindu temples at Madurai are covered with hundreds of thousands of terracotta figures of gods, supplicants, angels, and animals—a Hindu worship melée. They are all freshly painted every twelve years, which is no small feat in itself.

This brightly colored Ayyanar horse from southern India is now in the Tropenmuseum in Amsterdam, the Netherlands.

The patinated pieces with faint paint residues are our favorites. It takes a few monsoons to temper the vivid colors.

For more details about Indian art, please visit: www.mgroupstuff.com/indianart

OPPOSITE From the moment we bought this Ayyanar horse in southern India to the day the container arrived in the driveway, I worried about the fragile terracotta treasure. But it arrived intact—a miracle, given its large size and hollow kiln-dried clay construction. A bit of advice: Back away from the door when the padlock is cut and the container, which has been on a ship for three months, is opened. The wave of fetid Mumbai air almost knocked me out.

**NAME:** Protest art

**DATE:** United States, twentieth century

We found our "I Am a Man" placard in a brown sea of wonderful old books and manuscripts a few years ago at the New York Antiquarian Book Fair at a benefit for the New York Public Library. Bright red and white, it was such a relief to see something from a century I had lived in. And the message! The placards were carried by the Memphis Sanitation Workers in 1968 when they were on strike against dangerous work conditions and low pay. It was one of the most important events of the Civil Rights Movement and it continued for two months. Civil rights leader Martin Luther King, Jr., was in Memphis to speak to the strikers when he was killed.

Shown in this suffragette march in 1911, Miss Clemence Houseman gained fame as the first woman imprisoned for refusing to pay her taxes, pending her right to vote.

In 1967, lesbian activist Kay Tobin Lahusen documented a Philadelphia protest. Her archives of photographs of the gay rights movement are a treasure at the New York Public Library.

This great-looking feminist, with her cigarette and poster, is a quintessential representation of New York University in 1970.

This photograph of the 1968 Memphis sanitation workers strike by the African-American photographer Ernest Withers, who documented life in the segregated South in the 1950s and 1960s, shows the last march lead by Dr. Martin Luther King, Jr.

We have spent a fair amount of time as volunteers at the New York Public Library, and have seen a lot of its vast collection of ephemera—things that were meant to be used or read once, and then thrown away. They tell a story and give insight into events that would otherwise just disappear. Ephemera is highly collectible. For a brief moment when I was 26 years old, I was the ephemera expert at the auction house, Christie's. I was promoted for the weekend from my job at the front counter when I mentioned to the president of Christie's East that I had a huge collection of postcards. The Brit must have thought I meant valuable, vintage turn-of-the-century cards, when I was actually referring to funny roadside-attraction–type cards that I had been buying since high school. And I did have lots. I dutifully represented the auction house at a weekend conference and turned back into a front counter scullery on Monday morning. The protest posters are powerful on their own, but when seen in context, being held aloft by very brave citizens, they confirm their place in our history.

This poster was designed in 1989 by artist Keith Haring, who died of AIDS in 1990. It was part of ACT UP New York, a group famous for its powerful graphics created by leading artists to bring attention to the AIDS crisis.

This poster is another graphic treasure from the ACT UP archives at The New York Public Library. The archives are fully digitized, online, and are a constant source of inspiration for today's artists, historians, and activists.

For more details about protest art, please visit: www.mgroupstuff.com/ephemera

OPPOSITE Our placard, "I AM A MAN," leapt out at me at the New York Antiquarian Book Fair. I snapped it up and gave it to Hermes. We have no issue with hanging pictures over bookcases—even when we have the luxury of space.

# This house, a few doors off Fifth Avenue in Manhattan, was the first project where we completely gutted everything from cellar to roof.

All that was spared was the landmarked limestone Beaux Arts front façade. After it was completed two fleeting years later, visitors who walked through, even though they knew everything was new, would never fail to exclaim when they got to the library: "What a wonderful room! Is it original?" "No," we would answer, "everything is new, remember?"

The clients, who were newlyweds, both threw themselves into the design process with enthusiasm. We had done their country house a few months prior and had also decorated a penthouse for him as a bachelor pad, so we all knew how to play together. And they played fast…real fast. Hermes developed a scheme that included two incredible, jaw-dropping staircases. The front stairs soar six floors and float free of the walls, ending in a large glass-and-mirrored lantern. On the parlor floor, the stairs are part of an oval hall with a barrel-vaulted ceiling that connects the living room to the dining room. The back stairs are an open metalwork spiral culminating in a double-height greenhouse that opens into the library and onto a walled terrace lined with ten-foot-high arbor vitae and a brick fireplace.

The clients expected children would be arriving—between his, and theirs, we clocked in at seven before they moved out again—so our layout allowed for a progression of public and private spaces, with children's and guest rooms sandwiched between the master bedroom and library floor. New York townhouses, even extra-wide ones like this, often feel artificially lit, but the presence of natural light, reinforced by the work of a great lighting design team, created a bright and natural feel.

A shopping trip to Paris netted us twelve fireplaces, a container of antiques, custom-made gilded-door hardware, new couture for her, and an invaluable quantity of inspiration. The house is a mix of Directoire and Art Deco. The surfaces and materials were kept simple, with mostly plaster and French limestone. Any inclination to gild this lily was resisted. The height of the ceilings throughout was very important, and every inch was treasured.

The double-height library is Hermes' triumph. With balconies on three sides, one of which is used as an office, it soars without dwarfing the rest of the space. The simple and bold ceiling design is as successful from the second level as from the ground floor. Maple paneling was used instead of a traditional walnut or mahogany. It was French-polished and manipulated to give it warmth and age, and yet it feels refreshingly modern.

At the housewarming, as I was basking in the glow of the accolades—perhaps because I was wearing a name tag with "The Decorator" written on it—I overheard the Richest Man in New York say to the Second Richest Man in New York, maybe with irony, "Why can't we live this way?" Before I could enjoy this lovely nugget, some idiot accidently bumped the "all off" button on the dimming system, forcing me to hurl myself through the assembled A-list, frantically groping for the controls. These things keep one humble.

OPPOSITE The first time we saw the house, the placard on the front door read, "Foundation for Manic Depression," which pretty much summed up the interior.

OPPOSITE The front hall carries some of the vestibule's hard-edged decoration further inside the house. The iron table was made by early twentieth-century French furniture designer Gilbert Poillerat for French shoe genius Roger Vivier's house in the south of France. It is flanked by a pair of Louis XIII armchairs. The painting is by Stephen Hannock.

RIGHT The landings on the upper floors each feature a large contemporary painting that overlooks the dramatic open space of the staircase. The tole and bronze lantern is one of a set of three that M (Group) designed. They are each hung on a single chain, and you never see more than one at a time as you ascend the stairway.

OVERLEAF The staircase designed by Hermes is a triumph, as it floats freely up the six floors and is bathed in light from a glass cupola. The mahogany handrail that has been set on Neo-Classical-style iron pickets was carved by hand on site.

RIGHT The double-height library is on the fourth floor of the house and does double duty as the sitting room to the adjacent master bedroom. Hanging over the Napoleon III-period red marble fireplace is a seventeenth century Dutch tile panel representing the world. Both were purchased on a Paris shopping trip.

1   *A cannon mounted as a lamp, England, nineteenth century.*

2   *Adjustable Regency reading table with leather top, England, early nineteenth century.*

3   *Napoleon III marble mantelpiece, France, 1860.*

4   *Delft tile map of the world, Holland, seventeenth century.*

5   *Art Deco leather club chairs, France, 1930s.*

6   *Pair of Louis XV fruitwood fauteuils, France, mid-eighteenth century.*

7   *Low puzzle table in eight pieces, China, early nineteenth century.*

LEFT The arched window opens onto a five-story-tall glass greenhouse that Hermes designed to house the secondary stairway, a French-blue open spiral that connects metal bridges that span the front and back sections of the house. The terrace has a large outdoor fireplace and is enclosed by a severe and effective nine-foot-tall hedge for privacy.

# NAME: Steel furniture and decorations
# DATE: Eighteenth to twentieth century

The iron and carbon alloy we call steel has been around for thousands of years. The earliest forges found in Sri Lanka date from about 300 BCE, powered by monsoon winds. Very clever. It wasn't until the mid-seventeenth century that production techniques allowed for larger-scale steel production and the opportunity to use the valuable metal for something other than sword- and knife blades. In the eighteenth century, Peter the Great established foundries to make armaments in the eastern Russian city of Tula. During the infrequent lulls in fighting, the factories began to produce household items for exceedingly grand households.

Peter the Great, painted by British artist Sir Godfrey Kneller in 1698, radiates power in his Tula steel armor.

This Napoleon III steel console table with a marble top would make a great bathroom vanity.

Horse armor, called barding, is exemplified in this seventeenth century steel equine cladding, complete with fiddlehead horns.

Empress Catherine the Great became a patroness of the elaborate Tula metalwork, which were covered in chiseled, diamond-like steel and mixed metals, such as gold, silver, copper, and brass. Tables and chairs, large chandeliers, and small parasol handles made of these metals were all prized. The Napoleonic wars saw the end of decorative work, and the factories of Tula returned to their militaristic roots. By Victorian times, steel evolved to Gothick or Rococo Revival to suit new tastes, and beautiful Art Moderne designs appeared in the twentieth century. We love the undecorated and totally functional Steelcase desks from the 1950s. Our personal steel journey began when I lurched out of a tiny, claustrophobic Parisian elevator and literally ran into an Athénienne at Fremontier, one of our favorite dealers. As the rest of the traumatized crew exited, we all gave each other the "We/you *have* to have this/them/that/those/him/her" look. Roman-style perfume braziers made for a French aristocrat with money to burn were now on their way to a new home in New York.

For more details about steel, please visit:
www.mgroupstuff.com/steel

**OPPOSITE** The glamorous Athéniennes were made in the late-eighteenth century in France and are very rare examples of steel furnishings. Originally, they were used for burning incense in an antique classical setting. The Coromandel screen, with its maroon-colored ground, accentuates the curved wall.

By the 1970s, Maison Jansen, the Paris decorating firm, had left its *ancien régime* roots behind and was almost exclusively creating contemporary designs like these steel and brass campaign chairs.

This Pop Art steel spiral staircase could have been on the set of the early 1970s television show, *Laugh-In*. That's a compliment.

RIGHT Some people see them as anachronistic, but Hermes and I like a big, and in this case, grand dining room. The architecture of the room was inspired by the French Empire and its decor continued the theme with classical acanthus patterns that have been embossed onto the custom-made silk velvet curtains, and act as gilded curtain-pole finials.The chandelier was a literal wreck when I found it in a corner of an auction house warehouse, but all the bits and pieces were in a bag, and when the restoration puzzle was complete, we had a huge, glittering nineteenth century piece of Swedish jewelry in the room. The Art Deco furniture has severe classic lines and, combined with the contemporary art, brings the room into the twenty-first century.

1 *Carpet, Tabriz, Persia, late-nineteenth century.*

2 *Set of 12 dining chairs by Andre Arbus, upholstered in Hermes leather, France, 1940s.*

3 *Console table in the manner of Andre Arbus, contemporary.*

4 *Fernando Botero, Still Life with Pears, acrylic on canvas, signed and dated 1964.*

5 *Cut glass and gilt-metal six-arm neo-classical chandelier, Sweden, early nineteenth century.*

6 *Art Deco macassar ebony sideboard with gilt-bronze mounts depicting the signs of the Zodiac, by Dominique (Andre Domin and Marcel Genevriere), France 1940s.*

7 *Alabaster and gilt-bronze sconces in the style of Jacques-Emile Ruhlmann, contemporary.*

ABOVE The master bedroom accom-
modates a Louis XVI mahogany
*bureau plat*, or desk, in a corner. The
eighteenth-century bedside tables are
made of Italian fruitwood.

ABOVE A brass-mounted mahogany chest of drawers and an armchair give the master bathroom a Russian furniture "theme." The chair has monogrammed terry-cloth slipcovers. The warm, gold marble is reflected in the walls of mirrors, which have neo-classical frames.

**NAME:** Empire style
**DATE:** 1810 to 1860

As the United States entered its adolescence in the nineteenth century, the fervor and optimism of the Revolutionary period was followed by two decades of harsh realities from a new form of government. There was a general lack of confidence in the new order, as well as a lack of credibility. But with the defeat of the British in New Orleans in 1815, the United States was again ascendant and optimistic. The big, brash Roman model of republic was followed by a more refined point of view that brought a period of neo-Grecian style.

George Washington in the Greek style was sculpted by Horatio Greenough as a Congressional commission in 1832. The controversial sculpture was in the Rotunda of the Capitol in Washington, D.C., for two years before being re-sited outside.

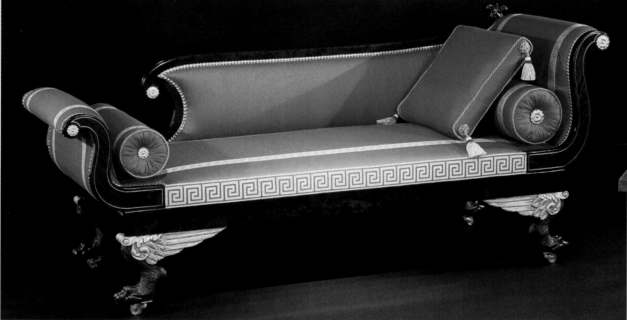

This opulent Duncan Phyfe sofa, with its sophisticated Greek-key frieze and winged feet, is very New York.

The beautiful, bright dining room at Edgewater has Duncan Phyfe furniture collected by financier Richard Jenrette, who bought the house from author Gore Vidal in 1969.

Edgewater, built in 1825 in Barrytown, New York, is a Hudson Valley historic treasure. The Grecian colonnaded façade fronts the wide Hudson River and the Catskill Mountains beyond.

The white-marble columns supporting this pier table are quintessentially Grecian. Made in Boston around 1818, the piece is a prime example of American neoclassicism.

New York furniture maker Duncan Phyfe, 1768-1854, was the ultimate resource for Manhattan's wealthy. A Scotch immigrant, Phyfe opened his studios in New York around 1800. His workrooms flourished quickly, furnishing the houses of New York's elite, and then exporting pieces to Philadelphia and cities in the South. Phyfe's restrained lines, pitch-perfect proportions, and elegant gilded mounts became synonymous with New York style. As his apprentices left to open their own firms, the

American Empire style reached the middle class. Bold and strong, the tables, chairs, cabinetry pieces, and mirrors commanded attention in any room. The Greek Revival era was long lived: It was dominant for 20 years and influential for 40 more. Of course, people need change, and what followed was a far cry from Greek Attic simplicity. The Victorian era saw revivals of elaborately decorated Renaissance and Gothic styles that continued into the beginning of the twentieth century.

For more details about American Empire, please visit: www.mgroupstuff.com/americanempire

**OPPOSITE** For a guestroom that faces a brick wall, Hermes designed a pair of large oval windows that I had covered in pleated silk. We included American Empire side tables and a great mechanical reading table. Opposite the bed is a huge, handsome American Empire *secrétaire*.

# Many moons ago, we got a call from the fanciest private bank in New York about one of their fancy Mexican clients.

They were considering a pied-à-terre at the Pierre Hotel in Manhattan, and we were on the short list of potential decorators. We happen to be great fans of the Pierre. We've worked in many of the great residential hotels in town and covet the life they offer. Room service. Hot and cold running staff. But of all the hotels, the Pierre has the best ceiling heights, the most gracious rooms, and incredible views of Central Park.

I'd actually been in the same apartment before, when it had been owned by Texans, and I had always thought it needed another public room. When we were hired, we voiced this concern, and about fourteen long months later, the hotel room next door was purchased to allow for a combination library-and-extra-bedroom and bathroom, momentarily achieving a Manhattan record for cost per square foot. If the *New York Times* had factored in the lawyers' bills, it would have remained the record.

The couple was very glamorous. He was tall and handsome, she was beautiful, and both had very refined tastes. In the end, they looked great in the apartment. The evening when the señora was sitting in the living room, wearing a red Lanvin dress with major Harry Winston diamonds, and her jet black hair in a tight chignon, she fit the room *perfectly*. I knew our work was complete.

Their Impressionist art collection spans the entire genre—whichever name you can think of, they had one or two. We kept the architecture simple but extremely detailed, and painted it about six different shades of ivory. The vestibule and front hall were done in a French Directoire scheme with a Mexican twist. We showed the clients two options of eighteenth-century–inspired decorations, including sunflowers with bees, or a neo-classical motif of intertwined corncobs and peppers. "Que? *Pimientos?!* Dios mio." So sunflowers it was. The apartment is extremely luxurious: pale, delicate, and full of treasures. It is an oasis—with room service.

OPPOSITE The Louis XVI-style building, with its iconic Mansard roof inspired by the Royal Chapel at Versailles, rises forty-two stories at the southeast corner of Central Park, facing the western sky. The hotel was completed in 1930, at the rocky beginning of the Great Depression, and within eight years was sold to J. Paul Getty and converted to its current 50/50 mix of private apartments and hotel rooms. That mix is a New York phenomenon—every elevator ride is rife with the potential to spot a movie star, potentate, or contemporary courtesan. Luxurious and fun.

**NAME:** Blue and white export porcelain
**DATE:** Fourteenth to nineteenth century

In the decorating world, blue and white is ubiquitous. It has been used as a motif and color scheme for centuries. Fresh, cool, and clean, we think it works best with a jolt of yellow or hot pink thrown into the mix. The blue and white phenomenon originated in China. Early traders from Persia brought cobalt to the Middle Kingdom, where it was considered twice as valuable as gold. The Chinese used the cobalt glaze first in the tenth century, but it came into its own in the fourteenth century, when higher quality and purer white porcelains better showed off the clear, intense blue.

A pair of large late-seventeenth-century Kangxi ginger jars with lids were decorated with court ladies.

In the nineteenth century, beautifully detailed paintings on silk, like this one of a Chinese junk, were exported. This little gem was a gift for my sixth-grade graduation, from a lady who obviously had an insight into my future.

The venerable German porcelain factories at Meissen have been making the ever-popular *Blue Onion* china pattern for over 300 years.

This incredible eighteenth century Canton-lacquered black-and-gold paneled room is overlaid with seventeenth century porcelains from the Vung Tau cargo, a sunken junk discovered by lucky fishermen off the coast of Viet Nam in 1990.

The first export market was back to Persia—the Chinese called cobalt "Persian blue"—and then it spread to the West. Europe became obsessed with the fine quality of the Chinese porcelains in the seventeenth and eighteenth centuries. The Germans and French industries were developmentally neck and neck at the beginning of the eighteenth century. François Xavier d'Entrecolles, a French Jesuit priest, smuggled the highly secret formula for porcelain out of China in 1712, along with information about silkworm production and artificial pearls—an example of how industrial espionage has been around forever. It is believed that the Polish king Augustus the Strong, 1670-1733, who bent horseshoes with his bare hands and fathered over 300 children, was also a patron of the arts and loved porcelain. He traded 600 of his most elite soldiers to the king of Prussia for some cash and 151 blue-and-white vases for his fantastic palaces in Dresden. Once the Europeans could make their own blue and white porcelains, Far Eastern exports fell precipitously, but the Chinese motifs remained. Meissen's *Blue Onion* and Minton's *Blue Willow* china patterns have been popular for 300 years. The Dutch created garnitures in the Chinese taste using the shapes and variations of the patterns from the Far East. The pagoda-shaped tulipières, with openings for multiple tulips, are a favorite form of ours, as they are tall and sort of wacky.

Rescued porcelains line tiny shelves and are even incorporated into the chandelier in this Parisian salon.

The Dutch loved their Delft pottery—and their tulips. These towering pagoda-inspired tulipières can display dozens of tulips.

For more details about Chinese Export porcelain, please visit: www.mgroupstuff.com/blueandwhite

**OPPOSITE** In the foyer, two blue and white Chinese Export vases stand in a Louis XVI marble-topped console that is flanked by a pair of Louis XVI painted and gilded side chairs. The painting, by French master Henri Matisse, is an obvious choice for an interior room that has no windows. The overdoors are made of basket-weave plaster overlaid with sunflowers and bees.

RIGHT For us, an apartment at "The Pierre" defines Manhattan luxury. It is a prime location, with beautiful and generously proportioned rooms with huge windows—assets other great residential hotels usually lack—serviced by a superior hotel staff. "Hi, room service. Two Diet Cokes, please." What's not to love? Add in a slew of French Impressionist paintings as a jumping-off point, and an off-white palette, and you have luxury. Right? We chose to run with the French inspiration when we designed the apartment. It feels like it's in the Pierre. The paneled living room opens onto a smaller library with an idyllic tropical Gauguin landscape. Seven whites subtly pick out the paneling details to ensure the room reads "white" but not "simplistic." Nothing is more luxurious in Manhattan than ivory silk and wool carpeting, woven in France on a narrow loom.

1 *Black lacquer and ormolu mounted Louis XV commode, France, mid-eighteenth century.*

2 *Louis XVI painted and parcel gilt fauteuil, France, mid-eighteenth century.*

3 *Amedeo Modigliani,* Jeune fille assise, les cheveux dénoués, *oil on canvas, France, 1919.*

4 *Edgar Degas,* Préparation à la danse, pied droit en avant, *original wax model executed between 1882 and 1895. This bronze version was cast between 1919 and 1921, France, twentieth century.*

5 *Pair of rare lacquer demi-lune tables, China, eighteenth century.*

6 *Paul Gauguin, untitled landscape, oil on canvas, France, around 1890.*

7 *Pair of contemporary giltwood mirrors, in the Chinese taste, designed by M (Group).*

8 *Pair of wucai, or five-color porcelain vases, China, nineteenth century.*

9 *Two figures of horse grooms/attendants, China, Ming dynasty, 1368-1644 CE.*

10 *One of a pair of Famille Rose porcelain vases mounted as lamps, China, eighteenth century.*

11 *Two-tiered side table with Japanned decoration, France, Contemporary.*

NAME: Amedeo Modigliani, 1884-1920

DATE: Late-nineteenth to early-twentieth century

Modern art includes many "isms"—Cubism, Surrealism, Futurism, Fauvism, and Dadaism—to name a few. But Italian painter and sculptor Amedeo Modigliani's work defied categorization. His beautiful portraits, with their elongated features and almond-shaped eyes, were influenced by his peers—the French Impressionist master Paul Cézanne, in particular—and by the new rage for *l'art primitif*, which embraced the art and artifacts of Africa.

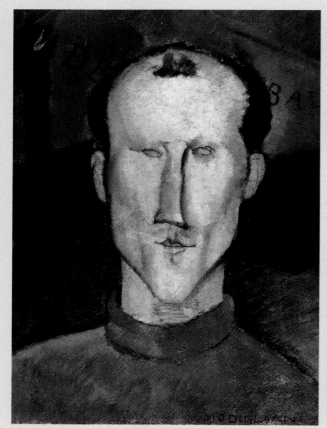

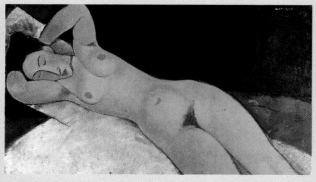

Modigliani's paintings of nudes scandalized the conservative Parisians in the early twentieth century. The police commissioner would vocally condemn the display of pubic hair.

Amedeo Modigliani was one of the artists who lived and worked in Montparnasse, Paris. His nickname, "Modi," is a play on *maudit,* which means accursed, in French.

The portrait of Leon Indenbaum, a Russian-born sculptor and fellow Montparnasse resident, was painted in 1915.

Modigliani's nickname in Paris in the teens was Modi, a play on the French term *peintre maudit,* or cursed artist. Handsome, brilliant, and sexy, he was the bad boy of the Montparnasse set. Between the hashish, cocaine, ether, and morphine, all of which he washed down with absinthe, his other addictions, and an incurable tuberculosis, he was indeed cursed. After only fourteen years in Paris, he died in the arms of his pregnant lover, Jeanne Hébuterne, who jumped to her own death a day later. It was a tragic *vie de bohème.* Modigliani was extremely prolific, sometimes producing hundreds of drawings in a day. But his work never sold well during his lifetime, and he was reduced to selling his paintings to people on vacation in the south of France. Times and tastes have since changed, and in 2010, his sculpture *Tête* sold for $59.5 million, and his paintings have price tags from over a million dollars to a record of $30 million. At Modigliani's funeral, Pablo Picasso, upon seeing police who had arrested the young artist so frequently, lining his funeral route, remarked: "Do you see? Now he is avenged." Since revenge is a dish best served cold, I would argue that the price *Tête* sold for is the best vindication.

This *Self-Portrait* of 1919 shows an effete and rather fragile-looking artist perched on a small, straight-backed chair.

Inspired by African art, Modigliani sculpted *Tête* between 1910 and 1912. In 2010, the limestone head sold at auction at Christie's in Paris for $59.5 million.

For more details about Amedeo Modigliani, please visit: www.mgroupstuff.com/modigliani

OPPOSITE An elegant late-eighteenth-century French chest has black and gilt panels and gilt metal hardware. A dancer by French artist Edgar Degas acts as an anchor for the Modigliani portrait behind it.

# The Gainsborough Studios is one of those legendary small New York buildings that people dream of living in.

On the southern border of Central Park, the famous double-height living rooms overlook Manhattan's great garden—and not from a lofty perch, but from an approachable point of view. The building, designed by American architect Charles W. Buckham, dates from 1907 and was originally developed as studios for affluent painters and sculptors. Our client at the time, and now one of our closest friends, had seen the apartment years before she actually bought it—she coveted it for a decade. When it came back on the market, she leapt, and our renovation began.

The apartment had been a bachelor pad in its last incarnation, with modern brass rails and black leather furniture. The first battle was deciding whether to paint the oak paneling or leave it stained. While we strongly advocated painting it, it was only once her friend—the well-known and very funny playwright Wendy Wasserstein—told her that the oak looked like "a Yale common room" that she admitted defeat and agreed to paint.

Not only did we want to bring the space back to its turn-of-the-twentieth century origins, we wanted to make it even better. We paneled the balcony and dining room in a complementary vertical form, replaced the staircase, and exchanged the modernist green-marble fireplace for a sixteenth-century French limestone surround. A total of eight pale, earthy khakis and greens were developed to emphasize the beams and paneling details in an effort to bring Central Park's natural palette inside.

Once we had created our ideal Old World environment, we brought it forward with pieces from our client's art and furniture collections, which we culled from her other homes in Paris, London, and Miami, as well as in Holmby Hills and Palm Springs, California. The space is bright, open, and huge, yet always cozy and comfortable. It is a grand space that people love being in. To us, it is quintessential New York.

OPPOSITE Central Park may be steps away, but be sure to look both ways before you take off across Fifty-ninth Street—it's treacherous. The apartment has a great view from a height that clears the tree line, but isn't so high you are completely removed from the action below.

RIGHT We think this was a true
trophy apartment. The beautiful large,
double-height living room looking
north over Central Park is intimate
and comfortable for a single person
and perfect—airy and big—for a
cocktail crush. It came to us with
oak paneling that bisected the room
and created a huge 'box without a
top.' Everything conspired to stop
the eye at a low horizon created
by the oak. Our first challenge was
to come up with a scheme that would
integrate the beamed ceiling into the
room below. Hermes added to the
paneling, and a palette of eight khaki
greens and beiges was developed to
make a unified room.

1 *Pair of mahogany "Ribbon" side
tables, designed by M (Group), contemporary.*

2 *Anglo-Indian boxes made from
tortoise-shell, rosewood with ivory
inlay, and porcupine quills.*

3 *Chinese-style black lacquer table
by Maison Jansen for the Jack Warner
villa, Villa Aujourd'hui, in Cannes,
France, 1950s.*

4 *Stacking lacquer boxes, Japan, late
nineteenth century.*

5 *A twelve-panel Coromandel screen,
purchased by William Haines for the
Jack Warner estate in Beverly Hills,
China, seventeenth century.*

6 *Phyllostachys nigra, black bamboo.*

7 *A pair of Anglo-Indian armchairs,
mahogany and caning, India, twentieth century.*

8 *"Cloud" card table, with a cork top
and mahogany legs, by Paul Frankl for
Johnson Furniture Company, United
States, 1950s.*

9 *"Plunging Neckline" side chair by
Paul Frankl for Johnson Furniture
Company, United States, 1950s.*

10 *Marcel Gromaire, Reclining nude,
France, 1930s.*

11 *Cigarette table in the form of a
camel, made of carved wood and
ivory inlay, Middle East, late nineteenth century.*

# NAME: Coromandel screens
# DATE: Seventeenth to twentieth century

Starting in the seventeenth century, the Coromandel Coast in southwest India was the first stop for Chinese treasures that would be headed to the West, hence the name of the big wooden folding screens we love that have been in grand and chic houses for five centuries now. Created by building up and incising multiple layers of lacquer, the earliest screens date from the end of the Ming period (1368-1644), reached their zenith in the early Qing period, late seventeenth century (1644-1912), and continue to be made today.

Close-up of a screen reveals the beautifully carved and colored details in one of the scenes.

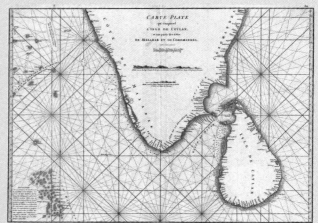

This detailed 1775 navigational chart of southern India and Ceylon by Jean-Baptiste d'Après de Mannevillette includes the Coromandel Coast, the site of centuries of conflict as England, Holland, France, and Denmark fought over access to its ports.

Rare in China, they were hugely valuable in Europe, and smaller pieces of Coromandel were incorporated into some of the greatest examples of eighteenth century-French furniture. Tastemakers in the twentieth century, such as fashion designers Coco Chanel, Yves Saint Laurent, and Valentino, loved and owned the screens. Ours is a nice one, dated 1688, and bought by Hollywood

The screen that flanks the fireplace in the living room in a New York apartment by M (Group) works beautifully with the mix of antique furniture and contemporary art.

decorator William Haines for movie mogul Jack Warner and his wife Ann's famously luxurious house in Beverly Hills, California. The best screens have amazing details: Each face is distinctive, and the gardens, pavilions, furniture, and rugs in the scenes were done from life. Later screens were less customized and used paper stencils to repeat faces. Screens can be tall and wide—over ten feet tall and up to sixteen-panels wide. The front is a view of a Chinese mansion, complete with concubines, children, and servants amid the lush scenery. The reverse is a graphic and elegantly gilded calligraphic homage to the patron. The favorite screen we found for a client was from Dalva Brothers, a venerable dealer of antique French furniture in New York. It is a dark, rich brown, decorated not with a scene but with a visual catalog of the owner's painting collection. Paintings, prints, and fans are saved for posterity, with the images sometimes spilling over from panel to panel. All this confirms the erudition and taste of the scholar who commissioned it. This very rare piece has it all—color, condition, provenance, and the bonus of a graphic, contemporary motif.

A Coromandel screen is seen in situ in a nobleman's house, in a seventeenth century woodblock print.

A rare Louis XV slant-top desk, with bits of Coromandel lacquer on an aubergine ground, came from Dalva Brothers.

For more details about Coromandel screens, please visit: www.mgroupstuff.com/coromandel

OPPOSITE This grand screen from our client's childhood home anchors the double-height–ceilinged living room. The side tables, by M (Group), were based on a classic Ming Chinese ribbon table. The black basalt urns were mounted as lamps by William Haines in the 1960s for a very swell weekend house in Palm Springs, California. The nineteenth-century Chinese Export figurines deserve a close look. Each was over-painted in the 1950s with crazy details by a Hollywood set designer. The armchair is one of a pair of Anglo-Indian reproductions from British Khaki. They were distressed and polished, and now they fool experts—not that that was our intent.

LEFT AND OPPOSITE Hermes designed the new woodwork to take the apartment back to 1907. His turned balusters and staircase, the balcony bookshelves, and the dining room walls all add details that reinforce the idea of a luxurious artist's studio from the beginning of the twentieth century. The sixteenth-century French limestone mantel gives the living room a grand scale. The carved bone-and-wood camel Syrian cigarette table, and the standing column lamp, were brought from the client's house in Palm Springs, California.

NAME: William Haines, 1900-1973
DATE: United States, 1920s to 1960s

One of our clients grew up in a Beverly Hills mansion decorated by William Haines, the legendary Hollywood designer. Thanks to this client's hand-me-downs, we've gotten up-close-and-personal with his work, and we absolutely love it. Billy, as he was known, rose from a silent-film bit player to become a major box office draw in the talkies. His film career ended with the oft-quoted Louis B. Mayer line, "You'll never work in this town again," after Haines chose his lover, Jimmie Shields, over a forced studio-lavender marriage. Their relationship lasted another fifty years. Haines and his business associate, Ted Graber, became stars in the design world. Billy was a brave guy.

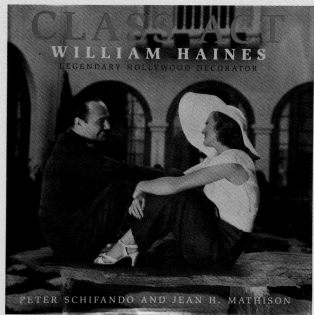

PETER SCHIFANDO AND JEAN H. MATHISON

**Published in 2005, *Class Act* is the definitive visual biography of the legendary Hollywood decorator.**

**Transforming sculptures into one-of-a-kind lamps became a Haines signature. Holes would sometimes be drilled into tables so that the cords would not be visible.**

**The signed publicity photograph of the handsome movie star was a favorite of his fans.**

**A 1955 drawing sketched the interior of Jack and Ann Warner's penthouse in New York.**

For decades, Haines successfully maneuvered through a minefield of difficult clients, including Joan Crawford, George Cukor, Jack Warner, Walter Annenberg, and Frank Sinatra. They all loved him. His clientele expected bespoke decoration, and he designed custom-made furniture and lighting for all his projects. His lamps were famous fantasies with vases, or *objets*, mounted on tall bases with wacky, and always very chic, shades. Billy invented the hostess chair, so the ladies of Hollywood could perch and pivot, ankles demurely crossed. The Warner screening room had sofas that mechanically reversed themselves so that the space could be reconfigured to watch the dailies. His style evolved constantly.

**In the living room of his own home in the fashionable Brentwood section of Los Angeles, Haines arranged his low, leather-covered chairs around one of his round tables.**

He was an early proponent of the elegant and theatrical Hollywood Regency style. He was always contemporary, with a lower case "c"—his rooms were modern and comfortable, and always flattering. Sunnylands, Walter and Lee Annenberg's phenomenal estate in Rancho Mirage, California, a Haines extravaganza, is now open to the public.

**Reproductions of the Brentwood or Hostess chair are available from William Haines Designs in Los Angeles.**

For more details about William Haines, please visit:
www.mgroupstuff.com/williamhaines

**OPPOSITE The view from the balcony is beautiful and offers a surprisingly different perspective than the living room below, as one looks down on the park instead of across it. With its wall of bookcases, the space functions as a sitting room for the guest bedroom and as a combination study-and-television-viewing room. The bright mustard-yellow leather club chair and the beautiful bronze Roman low-table, with its elaborately decorated eighteenth century-scagliola top, are by Haines.**

# This lady had dodged the M (Group) bullet for many years. We had done ten projects for her family, which included first- and second cousins and an aunt.

Those properties covered a large part of the east coast, from Maine to Florida. Finally, we were able to hook her: the big one. It bodes well when three of the staff in her very fancy building warn you on Day One that "Mrs. X is the most popular lady in the building." Picture a blond of a certain age, wearing a T-shirt that reads "Best *#$&@ Grandmother in Nantucket," big Schlumberger earrings, and a smile to match.

The apartment had been done ten years prior by one of America's great decorators. Everything was a dirty yellowish white, and the woodwork looked like it was from a Brooks Brothers outlet store. It started out looking old and never got much better. We rolled our eyes when she suggested a couple of quick fixes. I counter-proposed a gut job, and she agreed. Go figure.

This woman wanted fresh and happy. The first-floor location overlooking the tree-lined block makes the apartment feel like a townhouse. But like most townhouses, it needed more light. To paraphrase Billy Baldwin: The first person you hire is the lighting designer. We did, and it shows. Hermes attacked the spaces to raise the eye and square off things. Lame Colonial Revival was out and Severe Regency was in. Key entrances were raised to full height and highlighted; the less-important doors were incorporated into the wall paneling. The guest rooms and the master suite were detached from each other to give everyone a bit more privacy. A tiny unused terrace off the master bedroom was turned into an outdoor breakfast space. The spatial changes were minimal but very effective.

As we culled through her various houses and storage spaces, we hit pay dirt. There was stuff from her grandmother's house, which was famous for its 100 rooms, 125 servants, and six maroon Rolls Royces. Storage labels confirmed that these things had been in hiding since 1962. Not satisfied with the wealth of eighteenth-century materials, I complained, "I wish you had some black-and-white photos or *something* from the twentieth century. It's all so old and so grand." She piped up, "I have some photographs I've never framed, somewhere." A box was found and I pulled out the photo on top—it was a portrait of Constantin Brancusi by Edward Steichen, taken in 1922. When I picked myself up off the floor and dug further, I found forty prints that represented an overview of the history of photography from daguerreotypes to Mapplethorpe. "They were Daddy's." OK—we had a dining room theme. And there was lots of other good stuff: French miniatures, seventeenth-century porcelains, Disney cels.

One antiques dealer described this lady's post-La Caravelle-lunch shopping sprees with her *uber*-tasty brother as "the glory days when people bought beautiful things for fun, not to impress." Nothing makes for good decoration like great stuff. When all was said and done and ready for Christmas with her twenty plus grandchildren, the apartment was—like her—elegant, bright, colorful, and a bit subversive.

OPPOSITE Park Avenue is a legendary boulevard. From the 1920s, residential skyscrapers were built for families that previously owned single-family houses. Apartment dwelling became socially acceptable.

LEFT The vestibule has an eighteenth-century-Chinese column rug that was made to wrap around a stone pier for warmth. There is a border on only two sides, the top and bottom. The cabinet is an English Regency design. The cat sculpture that holds house keys is by the twentieth century Swiss sculptor Diego Giacometti. The black-and-white photographs, which include a portrait of movie star Marilyn Monroe, are all showstoppers.

OPPOSITE The pair of candle-stands in the hall outside the bedroom were brown mahogany when we found them in the client's storage space. They have since been water-gilded, which works with the period Regency candlesticks. I love a client who loves gilding. Watercolors by English book illustrator Arthur Rackham cover invisible doors and wall panels with scary fairy-tale images. A Rackham witch is a terrifying thing.

OVERLEAF The Regency pen-work chaise, with its fragile caning, is the drop-off point in the hall. A collection of eighteenth- and nineteenth-century embroideries is a testament to the talents and free time of the rich young women who sewed them. They are in their original frames, and some have hand-written signature labels.

JOHN BROOKES THE BOOK OF GARDEN DESIGN

Elements of Japanese Gardens by Isao Yoshikawa

JAPANESE RESIDENCES AND GARDENS

David Hockney

THE COMPLETE LANDSCAPE DESIGNS AND GARDENS OF GEOFFREY JELLICOE

TURKISH STYLE

ONE HUNDRED ENGLISH GARDENS Patrick Taylor

TIM STREET-PORTER THE LOS ANGELES HOUSE

DECORATION Condé Nast Books

HOLLYWOOD

**NAME:** Maison Jansen
**DATE:** France, twentieth century

For over 100 years, the Parisian firm Maison Jansen was the grandest of the grand in the decorating world. Jansen created interiors for kings and queens, shahs, and socialites. In the beginning, the style was very French and very ancien régime, eventually expanding to encompass more contemporary design. Regardless of the style, a piece of furniture or a room by Jansen always made a grand statement.

Mrs. John F. Kennedy hired the French firm to oversee her famous restoration and decoration of the White House.

An elegant dressing room in the French style was designed in the 1940s for one of my favorite houses in the El Country Club neighborhood of Havana.

A sketch depicts an outdoor seating area for one of the 54 guest pavilions built for the Shah of Iran's celebration in the desert at Persepolis.

Jansen's upholstered pieces combined eighteenth century elements with twentieth century scale and comfort. Signed pieces are very desirable and fetch high prices.

Maison Jansen had satellite offices all over the world. We spent a lot of time in Havana, Cuba, while Hermes wrote *Great Houses of Havana*, and I spent many hours sitting in a pre-revolutionary Jansen chair, waiting for appointments to see yet another grand house. The firm sent Cuban hardwoods back to France to make Louis XV-style furniture that could endure the heat and humidity. The ubiquitous Cuban rocking chair was gilded and reinterpreted in high French style to keep the rich Habañeros cool. Maison Jansen decorated the palaces and houses for the super-rich and planned their parties. The ultimate—literally, since the firm never financially recovered from it—was the Shah of Iran's 1971 celebration of the 2,500th anniversary of the Persian Empire.

The Tent of Honor at Persepolis was made of red Italian damask and sported eight Empire-style Bohemian crystal-and-gilt metal chandeliers.

The oval Blue Room at the White House was a Napoleonic masterpiece. General wear and tear and the subsequent design efforts of later First Ladies meant that the room would remain intact for less than a decade.

For more details about Maison Jansen, please visit: www.mgroupstuff.com/maisonjansen

**OPPOSITE** Two curved grass-green silk velvet sofas flank the fireplace and a Pierre Bonnard landscape. The 1950s ebonized and *verre églomisé*—or reverse painted glass—low table was made by Maison Jansen. The Louis XVI mantelpiece was the result of a fireplace field trip, a favorite project milestone for Hermes and me. Here, we needed only one; other jobs have needed a dozen. When we go to the big Parisian dealers we are stunned by the variety for sale and the speed with which the French porters showing them to us can hurl them around.

PRECEEDING PAGES
The room-sized antique Spanish rug was the element that drove the decoration of the living room. We believe that large is always better than small when it comes to rugs. The grass-green taffeta and silk velvet is a happy color, and the red lacquer secretary, and lots of black and gold accents give the room snap.

LEFT One of a pair of late-eighteenth century English Adam marquetry commodes, a collection of framed needlepoints, and an eighteenth-century mirror, also one of a pair, anchor one side of the living room. When I think a room is too formal, I stand back and leave it to the owner to add to it— or not. This lady added. It's more fun now.

OPPOSITE Given all the multiples of watercolors, photographs, and needlepoints, we felt we needed a couple of big, wall-sized images. Japanese screens are a favorite. This one, which depicts a lush landscape, functions as the cutting garden the living room was missing.

## NAME: Regency penwork
## DATE: Late-eighteenth to mid-nineteenth century

The English Regency period, between the Georgian eighteenth century and Queen Victoria's advent in 1837, saw great artistic and architectural achievements. It was a period of excess for the aristocracy, led by George III's heir, the profligate Prince Regent, who would not become King George IV until the ripe old age of 58. For thirty years, the unrestrained royal reigned over fashion. Prince George was not a cheap date. Definitely a man with taste, energy, and drive, he was over $100 million in debt before he was thirty years old. When he chose Brighton as the fashionable watering hole of choice, society followed. His Royal Pavilion set the benchmark for extravagant playhouses, blatantly ignoring the lessons that the recent French Revolution should have taught self-indulgent royals.

In Brighton, the Royal Pavilion's Mughal Indian exterior created a fashion for eastern exoticism.

A George III chinoiserie cabinet, *above*, features Oriental figures and pagodas as well as faux-Mandarin calligraphy painted in *grisaille* on its top, *below*.

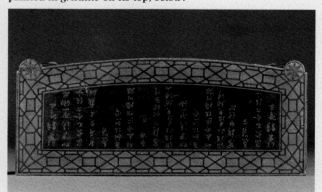

This magnificent penwork secretary pretty much says it all, as every surface has been decorated in polychrome or *grisaille*.

I've only been to the Brighton Pavilion once, when I was a graduate student at Oxford Universty, and I was blown away by a Regency-era theme park for the super-rich and painfully fashionable. I took the plebian train from London, and it turns out that the Brighton-London railway, opened in 1841, was the death knell for the royals' retreat, as hoi polloi like me descended on their seaside resort. As the British middle class grew, so did their need to emulate the swells. The luxurious and intricate wood, stone, and ivory inlays, and Asian lacquers in the furniture of the great houses of the aristocracy were reinvented for a broader market, via pen and ink. Taking the lead from the Prince Regent, the painted penwork furniture of the period was covered with fantastic landscapes, lithe Greek gods, and exotic Asian flowers, and drawn in white on black, black on white, or brown on gold, and then varnished to a golden yellow. The technique began in the seventeenth century and hit its zenith in the 1820s.

British artist Sir Thomas Lawrence captured the opulence of the era in his 1822 portrait of the Prince Regent, who later became King George IV.

The Banqueting Room in the Royal Pavilion featured five huge dragon-motif chandeliers suspended from a banana leaf ceiling medallion.

For more details about English Regency penwork, please visit: www.mgroupstuff.com/penwork

**OPPOSITE In the living room, an early nineteenth century Regency ivory-veneer sewing table is decorated with penwork. It has been paired with an ebonized, parcel gilt, and penwork Regency armchair.**

OPPOSITE The very rare secretary is an eighteenth-century Venetian *lacca povera* (poor lacquer) piece. Instead of hand-painting the decorations, paper cut-outs were glued to the wood and then covered with eight to ten coats of varnish. The collection of framed Walt Disney Studio cels includes scenes from *Snow White*, no less.

RIGHT The suite of miniature furniture has been tried out by many of the owner's grandchildren. The eighteenth-century Adam-style console is one of a pair.

RIGHT Hermes removed the "Park Avenue" (my quotes indicate disdain) base cabinets with bookcases, above, and designed curved-glass–fronted cabinetry for displaying her porcelains and rare books. The decorative painter sliced the pale grey walls with a razor blade to 'craze' the glaze. The strong gold and brown Oushak rug keeps the room from being too precious. The photography collection has maybe doubled since this picture was taken. The more the merrier.

1 *Apostle plate, one of a set, Germany, seventeenth century .*

2 *William Ordway Partridge, portrait bust, white marble, United States, late nineteenth century.*

3 *Edward Steichen,* Calla, *United States, early twentieth century.*

4 *Robert Doisneau,* Les Chiens de la Chapelle, *France, 1953.*

5 *Robert Capa,* Picasso and Child, *United States, mid-twentieth century.*

6 *Edward Weston,* Cabbage, *United States, 1931.*

7 *Ansel Adams,* Tree, *United States, 1948.*

8 *One of a pair of console tables, painted and parcel gilt, with marble tops, Italy, eighteenth century.*

9 *Carpet, Oushak, Turkey, late nineteenth century.*

**NAME:** John Marin, 1870-1953
**DATE:** Twentieth century

John Marin was an American modernist painter who, at the zenith of his career in the 1940s, was critically acclaimed as the "greatest living American artist." I was fifteen years old when I saw my first Marin painting. It was in one of my teacher's houses during my first year at boarding school. I didn't know anything about art, but I knew I liked what I saw.

Marin usually painted from life, or *en plein air*, as here at Cape Split, Maine.

From 1905 until 1917, the art world flocked to 291, Alfred Stieglitz's pivotal contemporary art gallery at 291 Fifth Avenue, in Manhattan.

Later, on field trips to the National Gallery of Art in Washington, D.C., I would seek out Marin's work. The immediacy and frenzied movement in his watercolors grabbed me then and continue to captivate me today. Marin first studied architecture and then went on to study art at the Pennsylvania Academy of Fine Arts in Philadelphia, and at the Art Students League of New York, and spent six years working and traveling in Europe. After his return to New York in 1909, Marin showed his work at 291, Alfred Stieglitz's legendary art gallery. The 291 clique included Georgia O'Keeffe—who was married to Steiglitz at Marin's house in Maine—Arthur Dove, Marsden Hartley, and Europeans such as Constantin Brancusi and Pablo Picasso. Stieglitz promoted African art, photography, poetry, and the arts in general. Marin divided his time between his homes in Cliffside, New Jersey, and Cape Split, Maine—both of which became subjects of his work. He felt you couldn't paint a place unless you knew it well. His post-1930s oils of the Maine coast and the Manhattan skyline were extraordinarily influential for the American Abstract Expressionist movement, and the work of the painters Jackson Pollock and Willem de Kooning.

The 1914 watercolor on paper is entitled *West Point, Maine.*

*Pine Tree, Deer Isle, Maine,* is a 1928 watercolor on paper.

The rocky coasts of Maine attracted American artists long before Marin took up residence there. Winslow Homer painted *High Cliff, Coast of Maine* in 1894.

For more details about John Marin, please visit: www.mgroupstuff.com/johnmarin

**OPPOSITE** A painting of a stormy coastline by American artist John Marin hangs on the library's gilded wallpaper. The needlework on the wing chair is old and probably original, which is something one doesn't see very often. Nor do you often see bright-green chinoiserie secretaries, like the one in the adjoining room.

# I live in one of the great buildings of Manhattan's Upper West Side. Built in 1908, it was the largest apartment building in the world for a moment.

The Belnord was completely state of the art, with underground driveways for deliveries, pneumatic tubes for messages to the front gate, and the largest courtyard in New York. The building occupies a full city block. The courtyard is our lobby, which connects the six elevator banks, or "halls" in Belnord-speak. There is a central garden fenced with chains, and cannon balls, and a big fountain with mounted eagles in the middle. It has a vaguely "Remember the *Maine*" memorial quality that I like. Very Left Bank on steroids. Only in New York.

My apartment is on a corner, looking up and across Broadway (which, if you had the energy and a few hours, would take you the 100 miles north to our house on the Hudson River and on to Canada). The front hall is generous and quirky, a real room. The doors are always open to the living and dining rooms, so there is a lot of great western light at the core. The windows are big even if the rooms aren't, and there is a strong feeling of space and light. There are two bedrooms—one for sleeping, and the other for dressing, which is a real blessing. The dressing room can handle a big desk, bookshelves, lots of floor space for bags waiting to go upstate, a chest of drawers, and a big Chinese cabinet. And when company comes, I can close the door. The walls are covered in cork—I could say, in homage to Proust, but I've never read him. It allows me a huge bulletin board for tacking up photos and ephemera, guilt-free. Everyone inevitably (and annoyingly) says it is their favorite room in the apartment. "It's like being in your brain," said one friend. "Scary...," she shuddered.

Like most of our work, the decoration is a balancing act. The high-gloss front hall feels slick and shiny, and leads into pale-blue grass-cloth–covered walls in the living- and dining rooms. These two rooms visually work as one space, with two rugs—one Persian and one French Modernist—delineating the rooms. The palette is a balance of warm camelhair and cool blues. We like mixing gold with silver, warm with cool. The floors are a deep Donald Kaufman brown/green deck paint that provides a strong grounding frame for the rugs and looks great with everything. We like our floors very dark or very light (white, even), but never in between.

OPPOSITE The landscaped courtyard has to be one of the best "lobbies" in New York. It is a constant source of pleasure, whether I am being dragged across it by Frankie or lingering on a bench.

LEFT The Aztec cactus—the invoice from the Throckmorton Fine Art gallery described it as a phallic symbol, but it looks like a cactus to me—stands on an eighteenth century Chinese stand, and is reflected in an American Empire giltwood mirror. The front hall beyond has a large canvas by contemporary American abstract painter Kathy Burge, an eighteenth-century Chinese center table, and a pre-Columbian stone shaman from Costa Rica.

OPPOSITE The living and dining rooms have the same grass cloth and paint colors. For us, it's all about flow and consistency. The Persian rug in the dining room is a calm foil to the Modernist one in the living room. The American Art Deco table in the dining room is ringed by M (Group)'s 440 chairs. The table is decorated with a pair of 1940s Mexican folk-art gourd cranes and assorted silver bowls filled with mosses and ferns. We found the French Art Deco sideboard in Hudson, New York, and it remains one of our best bargain finds.

NAME: Aztec culture

DATE: Mexico, 500 BCE–1492

Colima is a town on the Pacific Coast of Mexico. In pre-Columbian times, before 1492, the Aztecs buried the wealthy with food and objects made out of burnished clay for the afterlife. The objects are anywhere from 700 to 2000 years old. The little dogs, either fat and happy or fat and snarling, are the classic subjects. I found one I call Pancho Senior at the Winter Antiques Show in New York a few years ago from Spencer Throckmorton, one of my favorite pre-Columbian art dealers.

The monumental Olmec civilization head is now in the magnificent National Museum of Anthropology in Mexico City.

Funerary sculptures from Colima feature edibles—who doesn't crave crab in the afterlife? The crab form is rare. This one was a gift to Hermes but I had giver's remorse and took it back.

The image of an Aztec warrior is from one of the few surviving pre-Columbian documents, the beautiful 76-page Codex Borgia, in the Vatican Library in Rome.

An Aztec clay figurine depicts a servant carrying water and provisions for his master's next life.

The dogs, called Xolos, and pronounced *sho-tos*, were raised for ceremonial use and were multi-purpose as they were used for protection and they were an Aztec edible, hence their chunky builds. They were also used for warmth. Hairless, their body temperature is higher than that of a normal, hairy mammal. I once had a chihuahua, the original Pancho, and I can attest that he was a hot little animal. Anciently, the dogs were funereal offerings thought to represent the god Xolotl, the Mayan equivalent of the Greek demi-god Charon, who ferried souls across the River Styx to the Underworld. As an added bonus, after the loyal Xolo guided you, you could eat him… Although rare, the breed is becoming more popular, and was added to the American Kennel Club roster in 2011. As the Mexican national dog—culturally, if not literally—the breed has been treasured by

The 24-ton Aztec stone calendar was found in 1790 during the excavation for a new cathedral to be built on the site of the Aztec temples.

nationalist Mexicans, such as the famous artists Frida Kahlo and her husband, Diego Rivera. The Xolos were kept tragically busy escorting the dead to the afterlife after Cortés arrived in Colima in 1522. With the Spaniards came European diseases that killed over 90 percent of the indigenous population within a century.

Frida Kahlo, the twentieth century Mexican artist, was fond of Xolos dogs because they reputedly relieved chronic pain.

For more details about pre-Columbian art, please visit: www.mgroupstuff.com/precolumbian

OPPOSITE The screen in the dining room is late-nineteenth-century Japanese, with the recumbent *kitsune*, or fox, hiding in the ornamental grasses—just like in Upstate New York. The *kitsune* is a shape-shifter in Japanese mythology, but his fluffy tail often gave him away. My pre-Columbian pooch Pancho Senior keeps him company.

LEFT A nineteenth-century Chinese chest in the dining room serves as a bar, sporting my grandfather Lamont's German silver cocktail shaker and silver golf-club swizzle sticks. Silver julep cups are a Southern thing—and linen cocktail napkins could be. The "Repeal the 18th Amendment" napkins are a treasure—and only one set of about thirty that I've bought over the years. The cocktail motifs are beautifully hand-embroidered and include roosters (cocktails, get it?).

NAME: Henry Varnum Poor, 1887–1970
DATE: Twentieth century

Henry Varnum Poor was an American artist, craftsman, teacher, and architect who worked in many mediums, including painting, drawing, sculpture, murals, ceramics, and design. And he excelled at each one. Born in Kansas, he studied at Stanford University, the Slade School in London, and the Académie Julian in Paris. He spent his life teaching and studying. One of his greatest endeavors was co-founding the Skowhegan School of Painting and Sculpture in 1946 in Maine. Skowhegan's summer residencies have nurtured some of America's great artists, such as Ellsworth Kelly and Alex Katz.

The 1930 *Paris Self Portrait* shows the painter as a confident and already-established artist.

A sunny summer day in the Hudson Valley, New York, is the setting for the 1940 *Frisk and Sister in Open Window*.

The door surrounds and murals at the Justice Department in Washington, DC, are part of a set Poor painted for the Works Progress Administration. They are revolutionary images of the downtrodden and the legal system.

Poor designed residential projects for his friends, turning his staircases into fine art. The ones shown above date from 1920, 1966, and 1935.

Poor was also a potter. Some of his decorative tiles are on a façade of a building on East 72d Street in Manhattan.

I came across Poor by accident. A large landscape came up at an American paintings sale at Christie's, the auction house, when I was an underling at the front counter. I acquired it by fluke: The auctioneer threw out the bids above me due to improprieties—a family member of Poor's was trying to jack up the price—and it was suddenly, unexpectedly, mine. It was a huge bargain and I have never tired of his colorful view of the Italian vineyards. Poor's own home, "Crow House" in Rockland County, New York, is a rambling house in a picturesque gabled stone compound, embellished with his ceramics. While he only designed and built a few houses over four decades, he created each of them with the restraint of great art. All were in his neighborhood, for his savvy friends, like actor Burgess Meredith. His staircases are treasures. Henry Poor fits into that category of hugely talented but not hugely commercial artists. In the art market, look for primary works by secondary artists rather than secondary works by primary artists. And don't even think about tertiary.

One of Poor's rare ceramic stoves has a design of leaf motifs.

For more details about Henry Varnum Poor, please visit: www.mgroupstuff.com/poor

**OPPOSITE** In a corner of the dining room, a ceremonial mask from Papua New Guinea shares a Chinese stand with a little parrot from Parisian taxidermist Claude Nature. The still-life of a pipe and peaches by Poor has a wonderful *sgraffito* (or scratched) frame, also by the artist.

RIGHT I treasure the six-foot-tall by five-foot-wide windows set in the two-feet-deep exterior walls—a testimony to pre-World War I construction methods.

1 *Beethoven mosaic by the Ravenna Mosaic Company, New York, 1930s.*

2 *Ivory-and-bone inlaid side tables, India, late nineteenth century.*

3 *Mask, Baule people, Ivory Coast, Africa, twentieth century.*

4 *Louis XVI-style painted* bergère, *France, twentieth century.*

5 *Pair of tie-dyed* pelangi *textiles, Indonesia, early twentieth century.*

6 *Gilt-iron and mahogany two-tiered side tables designed by M (Group), contemporary.*

7 *Pair of blue-and-red-glazed large baluster vases mounted as lamps, China, twentieth century.*

8 *Carved wood and painted dancing figure, south India, twentieth century.*

9 *Gilt-wood "Chinese ribbon" low table designed by M (Group).*

10 *Art Nouveau silver plated cigar holder, France, nineteenth century.*

11 *Pre-Columbian terracotta crab, Colima, Mexico, 500-1,200 CE.*

12 *Vincenc Vingler,* Monkey, *lead sculpture, Czechoslovakia, mid-twentieth century.*

13 *Sculpture stand, Chinese, eighteenth century.*

14 *Scholar's rock, Chinese, twentieth century.*

15 *Pair of ebonized and gilded Napoleon III-style slipper chairs, American 1940.*

16 *Art Moderne carpet, France, 1930s.*

17 *Frankie.*

**NAME:** Dianne Kornberg

**DATE:** Twenty-first century

We first saw contemporary artist Dianne Kornberg's work at Manhattan's Norha Haime Gallery in 1994. We were drawn to her large-scale photograph, *Twelve Cats*, which depicted a mass of fragile feline bones in bold Abstract Expressionist style. Her *Bone Stories* photographs were studies of the contents of boxes of materials from the botany department at Reed College in Portland, Oregon, which had been in storage since the 1930s. Many of Kornberg's pieces are diptychs, where the top of the box and the often cryptic label is one element, flanked by the open box and its contents as the other. The preserved feathers, bones, and butterflies are even more interesting when shown in their archival context.

The artist is shown in front of *Twelve Cats*, a 1992 work, from the series entitled *Bone Stories*.

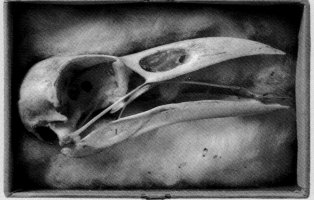

*Cartwheel 4* has a macabre joy. Kornberg says the juxtaposition of the skeletal materials doing a cartwheel suggests *carpe diem*, seize the day.

*Raven Skull*, a 1993 diptych from the Comparative Anatomy series, shows the interplay between the specimens and the packaging. The boxes, wrappings, and labels, in spidery script with postage stamps, are as important as the contents.

It looks like the elements—the bones—of our *Twelve Cats* were recycled in her subsequent *Strings* series. As beautiful, ethereal patterns of threads and tiny cat bones create grids, Kornberg's contemporary vision transforms the bones into brush strokes, creating art that transcends the materials. Kornberg photographed algae in her *Cors Mortale*, or *Mortal Heart*, series, creating her own Latin nomenclature for the plant life. Science and art, fact and imagination, and life and death all come together in her work. Her work echoes the earlier work of Anna Atkins (1799-1871), who is considered to be the first female photographer. Atkins' book *Photographs of British Algae – Cyanotype Impressions*, published in 1843, was the first book to feature photographic illustrations. Atkins' work was elegant and informative. Only seventeen copies of her self-published book are known to currently exist, though hundreds of the images can be found online at The New York Public Library Digital Gallery.

"India Tiger 5," 1995, Selenium-toned gelatin silver print and archival pigment inkjet prints. From the series "India Tigers."

For more details about Dianne Kornberg, please visit: www.mgroupstuff.com/diannekornberg

**OPPOSITE** The white marble rabbit, the sculpture stand, and the *gongshi* scholar's rock are all nineteenth-century Chinese. The chair is French, from the 1970s, and the blue rhinoceros-shaped garden stool is early twentieth-century faience. The photograph, by Kornberg, is framed in an oversized white lacquer frame that seems to allow the image to expand.

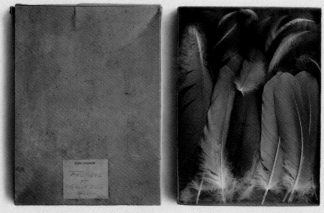

"Feathers of the Great Blue Heron," 1993, Cibachrome diptych. From the series "Comparative Anatomy."

**NAME:** Eugene O. Goldbeck, 1892–1986
**DATE:** Twentieth century

I discovered E.O. Goldbeck when I was a college student in San Antonio, Texas. At a BBQ restaurant, mounted above the benches where large families waited for tables, were stacks of really long, amazing photographs of cities and groups of people: Moscow's Red Square, the Havana harbor, thousands of soldiers, circus acts, high school classes, and bullfights. They were historic documents, full of details. I never went back to that restaurant, but I pulled out the White Pages and went to meet Goldbeck, the octogenarian photographer, and bought a slew of his prints for about 15 to 30 dollars apiece.

The Kodak Cirkut camera, introduced in 1907, had a mechanism that rotated it 360 degrees and used film that was up to 20 feet long.

*The Living Air Service Insignia, San Antonio, Texas,* shot near Kelly Field in 1926, was the first panoramic design Goldbeck took with real people creating the graphic shape.

Goldbeck was prolific. The Harry Ransom Center at The University of Texas at Austin has more than 1,000,000 items in their Goldbeck archives, including 70,000 prints. He traveled the world with his rotating Cirkut camera, and spent a lot of time photographing the United States military. His most-published image is of an Air Force insignia made up of 21,765 men taken in Lakeland AFB, Texas, in 1947.

The New York Yankees were photographed in San Antonio, Texas, on March 31, 1924.

Goldbeck hangs long prints to dry. I visited him in his studio around 1976, when I was a college student.

This group of men, and one woman, was taken in 1917. Like so many vintage photographs, the occasion and reason remain a mystery.

The prints are a lot of bang for the buck. Between 48- and 72-inches long, they are not cheap to frame but they are cheap to buy. The photographer's vintage signed prints start at 1,500 dollars apiece and peak at around 5,000 dollars. The new ones are only 100 dollars each.

Goldbeck was not acrophobic. Over his long career, he built many towers and wasn't shy about grabbing his subjects' attention—no small feat when he was dealing with up to 22,000 people.

THE PANORAMIC PHOTOGRAPHY OF
**EUGENE O. GOLDBECK**

By CLYDE W. BURLESON and E. JESSICA HICKMAN

The 1986 monograph on Goldbeck by Clyde W. Burleson and E. Jessica Hickman, published by the University of Texas Press, includes four-page fold-out panoramic images.

📱 For more details about E.O. Goldbeck, please visit: www.mgroupstuff.com/goldbeck

**OPPOSITE** Three panoramic Goldbeck photographs hang in the master bedroom over a red-lacquer Chinese chest. The small photograph of insects is by Dianne Kornberg, and the Aboriginal bark dot-painting dates from the late 1950s.

LEFT I threw the television into the art-wall mix of the master bedroom, making sure the art was in a variety of media—backlit movie-theatre advertisements, black-and-white- and color photographs, works on paper, an Aboriginal bark painting, and an Anglo-Indian painting on ivory. The cork-topped mahogany sideboard is by mid-century American designer Paul Frankl and was included in his collection for the Johnson Furniture Company.

OPPOSITE The dressing room has cork-covered walls, allowing for memorabilia—and lots of it. The chest of drawers is a good example of French nineteenth-century Charles X furniture. The photograph is by American artist Jean Pagliuso. The plaster cast of a modest Venus is "dressed to the nines" (there were nine Greek muses) in her plastic Mardi Gras beads, cultured pearls, and protest buttons.

# ESOTERICA

**NAME:** Anatomical models
**DATE:** Eighteenth century to today

I haven't touched a medical textbook since I was about eight years old, when I innocently opened a tome on skin diseases in my pediatrician's office. Innocence was quickly lost, and any thoughts of a medical career immediately evaporated. Who wasn't intrigued by those transparent "I am Man" and "I am Woman" models? They were like Barbie and Ken without clothes—or skin. Who didn't groan when the Periodic Table roller-shade came down in science class? These were tools for learning, or in my case, Pavlovian signals to tune out. Educational stuff, especially post-schooldays, is cool, and sort of dirty. Or is that just me?

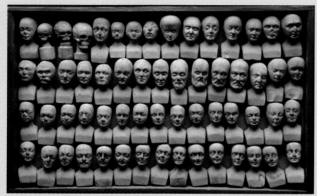

This collection of 60 tiny nineteenth century heads is from the Science Museum in London, England. Phrenologists believe the shape of the head determines personality, so this box must have come in handy in Victorian England.

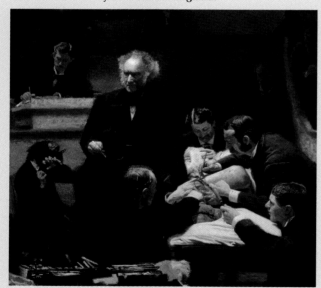

Sold for $68 million, Thomas Eakins' 1875 *The Clinic of Dr. Gross*, has been called the finest American painting of the nineteenth century by some people who really know what they are talking about.

The almost life-sized models feature organs that are removable. I would advise any adult to play around with one. Suddenly, the gall bladder in your hand becomes a reality, for better or worse. We prefer a bit of patina, so we opted to buy the manhandled vintage models, but new ones are easily available. One website I found offered an animal cell model at 20,000 times life-size and a ¾ life-sized human leg. There is truly something for everyone. Before there were plastic models, doctors depended on the living to provide learning experiences. The American artist Thomas

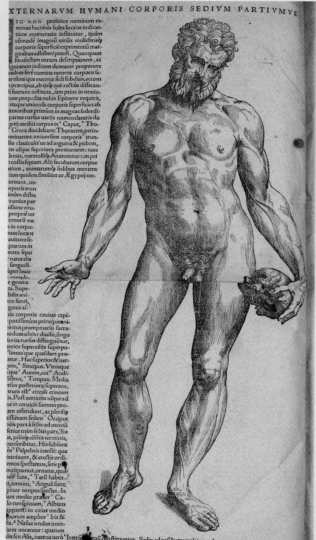

Flemish anatomist Andreas Vesalius, 1514-1564, published his *De humani corporis fabrica* or *On the structure of the human body*, when he was 29 years old in 1543. Brown University's copy is covered in human skin—maybe too much information?

Eakins' great 1875 painting *The Gross Clinic* graphically merged art and science. Eakins bucked the system and allowed women and men to share nude models in his classes, and practiced what he preached when he posed as a model himself. "Anatomie clastique" (from the Greek *klastos*, "broken in pieces") were created by French firm Maison Auzoux in the early nineteenth century, using accurately painted paper-mâché human and animal models. In the eighteenth century, wax was the preferred medium.

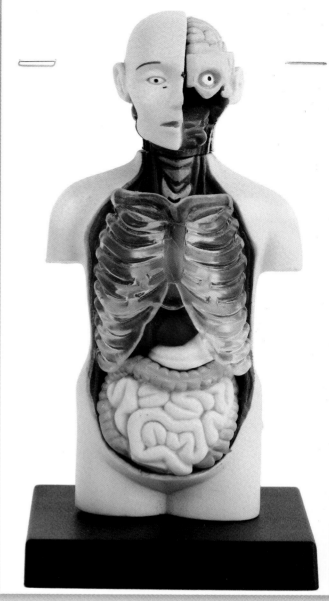

This tiny rubber model would be useful for a doctor's house calls, if such things still existed.

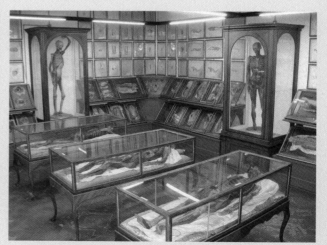

La Specola, the Museum of Zoology and Natural History in Florence, Italy, has a collection of 1,300 anatomical wax models of the human figure by the artist Clemente Susini, 1754-1814.

For more details about anatomical models, please visit: www.mgroupstuff.com/anatomicalmodels

**OPPOSITE** The bathroom, with its large biology-class instructional model, is focused on male body parts in photographs, plaster and plastic sculptures, and random postcards. All of these naked bodies inspire good hygiene.

210

Allan, Lois. *Contemporary Art in the Northwest.* New York: Craftsman House, 1995.

Archer Abbott, James. *Jansen.* New York: Acanthus Press, 2006.

Archer Abbott, James. *Jansen Furniture.* New York: Acanthus Press, 2007.

Attenborough, David. *The Tribal Eye.* BBC, 1976.

Barlow Rogers, Elizabeth. *Landscape Design: A Cultural and Architectural History.* New York: Harry N. Abrams, Inc., 2001.

Beard, Geoffrey. *The Work of Robert Adam.* London: Bloomsbury Books, 1987.

Belger Krody, Sumru. *Flowers of Silk & Gold: Four Centuries of Ottoman Embroidery.* Washington, D.C.: Merrell Publishers Limited, 2000.

Benjamin, Roger. *Icons of the Desert: Early Aboriginal Paintings from Papunya.* New York: Cornell University, Herbert F. Johnson Museum of Art, 2009.

Bennett, Ian, ed. *Complete Illustrated Rugs and Carpets of the World.* New York: A & W Publishers, Inc., 1977.

Bérinstain, Valérie, Susan Day, Élisabeth Floret, Clothilde Galea-Blanc, Odile Gellé, Marine Mathias, and Asiyeh Ziai. *Great Carpets of the World.* Paris: The Vendome Press, 1996.

Bony, Anne. *Meubles et Décors Des Années 40.* Paris: Editions du Regard, 2002.

Bowe, Patrick, Nicolas Sapieha, and Franceso Venturi. *Houses and Gardens of Portugal.* New York: Rizzoli International Publications, Inc., 1998.

Brawer, Nicholas A. *British Campaign Furniture: Elegance under Canvas, 1740-1914.* New York: Harry N. Abrams, Inc., Publishers, 2001.

Bricker Balken, Debra. *John Marin: Modernism at Midcentury.* New Haven and London: Yale University Press, 2011.

Burleson, Clyde W., and E. Jessica Hickman. *The Panoramic Photography of Eugene O. Goldbeck.* Austin: University of Texas Press, 1986.

Caruana, Wally. *Aboriginal Art.* New York: Thames & Hudson, Inc, 1993.

Chatwin, Bruce. *The Songlines.* New York: Viking Penguin, Inc, 1988.

Chenevière, Antoine. *Russian Furniture: The Golden Age, 1780-1840.* New York: The Vendome Press, 1988.

Cheronnet, Louis. *Jacques Adnet.* Paris: Art et Industrie, 1948.

Chiu, Melissa, and Zheng Shengtian. *Art and China's Revolution.* New Haven and London: Yale University Press, 2008 / Published in conjunction with The Asia Society, New York.

Cooper, Ilay and Barry Dawson. *Traditional Buildings of India.* New York: Thames & Hudson, Inc., 1998.

Couldrey, Vivienne. *The Art of Louis Comfort Tiffany.* New Jersey: The Wellfleet Press, 1986.

Dickson, Harold E., and Richard Porter. *Henry Varnum Poor: 1887-1970.* Pennsylvania: The Pennsylvania State University Museum of Art, 1983.

Dongerkery, Kamala S. *Interior Decoration in India: Past and Present.* India: D.B. Taraporevala Sons & Co. Private Ltd., 1973.

Ecke, Gustav. *Chinese Domestic Furniture.* Vermont: Charles E. Tuttle Company, 1962.

Eidelberg, Martin, Nina Gray, and Margaret K. Hofer. *A New Light on Tiffany: Clara Driscoll and the Tiffany Girls.* New York: New York Historical Society, 2007.

Emil Willers, Karl. *Milton Avery & the End of Modernism.* New York: Samual Dorskey Museum of Art, 2011.

Fiell, Charlotte and Peter Fiell. *Decorative Art: 50's.* Köln: Taschen, 2000.

FitzGibbon, Kate and Andrew Hale. *Ikat.* London: Lawrence King Publishing, 1997.

Fleischmann, Melanie. *In the Neoclassic Style: Empire, Biedermeier and the Contemporary Home.* New York: Thames & Hudson, Inc., 1996.

Gide, André. *Travels in the Congo.* New York: Penguin Books, 1986.

Hamlin, Talbot. *Greek Revival Architecture in America.* New York: Dover Publications, Inc., 1944.

Harmon, Katharine. *The Map as Art: Contemporary Artists Explore Cartography.* New York: Princeton Architectural Press, 2009.

*Henry Varnum Poor: Paintings.* New York: James Graham & Sons, Inc., 1999.

Hu, Kemin. *The Spirit of Gongshi: Chinese Scholar's Rocks.* Massachusetts: L.H., Inc., 1998.

Isaacs, Jennifer, ed. *Australian Dreaming: 40,000 Years of Aboriginal History.* Sydney: Lansdowne Press, 1980.

Jay, Ricky. *Learned Pigs & Fireproof Women: Unique, Eccentric and Amazing Entertainers.* New York: Farrar, Straus and Giroux, 1986.

*John Hall and the Grecian Style in America.* New York: Acanthus Press, 1996.

Jourdain, Margaret and R. Soame Jenyns. *Chinese Export Art in the Eighteenth Century.* Middlesex: Spring Books, 1967.

Kaufman, Donald, Christine Pittel, and Taffy Dahl. *Color and Light: Luminous Atmospheres for Painted Rooms.* New York: Clarkson N. Potter, Inc., 1999.

Kemp, Martin and Marina Wallace. *Spectacular Bodies.* London: Hayward Gallery Publishing, 2000.

Kennedy, Jean. *Here is India.* New York: Scribner's, 1945.

Kennedy, Roger G. *Greek Revival America.* New York: Stewart, Tabori & Chang, Inc., 1989.

Kornberg, Dianne. *Field Notes: Photographs by Dianne Kornberg, 1992-2007.* Oregon: Marylhurst University, 2007.

Linley, David. *Extraordinary Furniture.* New York: Harry N. Abrams, Inc., 1996.

Long, Christopher. *Paul T. Frankl and Modern American Design.* New Haven: Yale University Press, 2007.

Lovatt-Smith, Lisa. *Moroccan Interiors.* Köln: Taschen, 1995.

McCorquodale, Charles. *History of the Interior.* New York: The Vendome Press, 1983.

Madden, David. *The Authentic Animal: Inside the Odd and Obsessive World of Taxidermy.* New York: St. Martin's Press, 2011.

Makower, Joel, ed. *The Map Catalog: Every Kind of Map and Chart on Earth and Even Some Above It.* New York: Vintage Books, Tilden Press, 1993.

*Mallett: Exceptional Furniture and Works of Art.* London: Mallett, 2011.

Mann, William J. *Wisecracker: The Life and Times of William Haines, Hollywood's First Openly Gay Star.* New York: Viking Penguin, 1998.

Marion, John. L. *The Best of Everything: The Insider's Guide to Collecting—For Every Taste and Every Budget.* New York: Simon and Schuster, 1989.

Mendelson, Cheryl. *Home Comforts: The Art and Science of Keeping House.* New York: Scribner, 1999.

Midant, Jean-Paul. *Art Nouveau in France.* Paris: Books & Co., 1999.

Miller, Judith. *Tribal Art.* London: Dorling Kindersley Limited, 2006.

Michell, George and Antonio Martinelli. *The Royal Palaces of India.* New York: Thames & Hudson, Inc., 1994.

Moore, Derry. *Evening Ragas: A Photographer in India.* London: John Murray, Ltd., 1997.

Monti, Franco. *African Masks.* Middlesex: The Hamlyn House, Ltd., 1969.

Mowry, Robert. D. *Worlds Within Worlds: The Richard Rosenblum Collection of Chinese Scholars' Rocks.* Cambridge, Massachusetts: Harvard University Art Museums, 1997.

Myers, Bernard S. and Trewin Copplestone, eds. *Prehistoric and Primitive Man.* New York, London: McGraw Hill Book Company, 1967.

Nakashima, Mira. *Nature, Form & Spirit: The Life and Legacy of George Nakashima.* New York: Harry N. Abrams, Inc., 2003.

Nelson, Peter. *Treehouses: The Art and Craft of Living Out on a Limb.* Boston, New York: Houghton-Mifflin Company, 1994.

*Neo-Classical Art Moderne Furniture, Part Two.* Sotheby's York Avenue Galleries, February 5, 1981.

Newton, Douglas. *Masterpieces of Primitive Art.* New York: Alfred A. Knopf, 1978.

*Oriental Art: Volume XLIV, Number 1,* 1998.

Paine, John A. *Sculptural Plaster-Casts in Halls 6, 7, 8, 9, 10 and 11.* New York: Metropolitan Museum of Art, 1840-1912.

Papathanassopoulos, Dr. G. *The Acropolis: A New Guide of the Monuments and Museum.* Athens: Krene Editions, 1991.

*Penwork: The Triumph of Line.* New York: Hyde Park Antiques, 1989.

Pilcher, Donald. *The Regency Style: 1800 to 1830.* London: B.T. Batsford, Ltd., 1947.

Piña, Leslie. *Fifties Furniture With Values.* Pennsylvania: Schiffer Publishing, Ltd., 1996.

Praz, Mario. *An Illustrated History of Furnishing.* New York: George Braziller Publishers, 1964.

Pushpanath, Salim, and Ajay Marar. *Kerala: Colours, Culture & Lifestyle.* Kerala: DeeBee Info Publications, 2000.

Quinn, Stephen Christopher. *Windows on Nature: The Great Habitat Dioramas of the American Museum of Natural History.* New York: Abrams, 2006.

Rennie Short, John. *The World Through Maps: A History of Cartography.* Toronto: Firefly Books, Ltd., 2003.

Rodgers, Dorothy. *The House in My Head.* New York: Atheneum, 1967.

Roehm, Carolyne. *A Passion for Blue & White.* New York: Broadway Books, 2008.

Sandwith, Hermione, and Sheila Stainton. *The National Trust Manual of Housekeeping.* London: Penguin Books Ltd., 1984.

Schinz, Marina, and Gabrielle van Zuylen. *The Gardens of Russell Page.* New York: Stewart, Tabori & Chang, 1991.

Sekler, Eduard F. *Josef Hoffmann.* New Jersey: Princeton University Press, 1985.

Shixiang, Wang, and Curtis Evarts. *Masterpieces from the Museum of Classical Chinese Furniture.* Tenth Union International, 1995.

Shixiang, Wang. *Connoisseurship of Chinese Furniture: Ming and Early Qing Dynasties.* Hong Kong: Joint Publishing (H.K.) Co., Ltd., 1990.

Sutton, Peter, ed. *Dreamings: The Art of Aboriginal Australia.* New York: George Braziller Publishers, 1988.

*The Last Empire: Photography in British India.* New York: Aperture, 1976.

*The Woodbook.* Köln: Taschen, 2002.

Thorne, Martha, ed. *David Adler, Architect: The Elements of Style.* New Haven and London: Yale University Press, 2002 / Published in conjunction with The Art Institute of Chicago.

Troost, J. Maarten. *Getting Stoned with Savages: A Trip Through the Islands of Fiji and Vanuatu.* New York: Broadway Books, 2006.

Watkin, David and Tilman Mellinghoff. *German Architecture and the Classical Ideal.* Massachusetts: The MIT Press, 1987.

Weisberg, Gabriel P. *Art Nouveau Bing: Paris Style 1900.* New York: Harry N. Abrams, Inc., 1986.

Wharton, Edith and Ogden Codman, Jr.. *The Decoration of Houses.* New York: W.W. Norton & Company, Inc., 1978.

Wills, Royal Barry. *Tree Houses.* Boston & New York: Houghton Mifflin Company, 1957.

Witt-Doerring, Christian, ed. *Josef Hoffmann: Interiors 1902-1913.* Munich: Prestel Verlag, 2006.

# ACKNOWLEDGMENTS

It goes without saying that in each of our lives, our success and our happiness are the sum of the influences and support of many, many people. Hermes and I sincerely thank our legions of friends and colleagues for three decades of professional and personal Fun.

## Hermes Mallea, my partner
*Whose taste, talent, erudition, encyclopedic memory, patience, and sense of humor never cease to amaze me after thirty years.*

## Betty Leaf, my mother
*Who taught me by example and encouraged me to see the world.*

## Our Clients
*Smart, generous, house-proud, and, without exception, nice people.*

## M (Group)
*A talented, hardworking, and charming bunch.*
*And to Patrick Hannon, in particular.*

## The Art and Antiques Dealers who shared their expertise and enthusiasm
*Robert Aronson, Aronson Antiquairs, Amsterdam*
*Ray Attanasio, Balsamo, New York*
*Martine Baverel, Galerie Vallois, Paris*
*Nader Bolour, Doris Leslie Blau, New York*
*David Cruz, Blackman Cruz, Los Angeles*
*David Dalva, III, Dalva Brothers, Inc., New York*
*Douglas Dawson, Douglas Dawson, Chicago*
*Paul Donzella, Donzella 20th Century Gallery, New York*
*Patrick Dragonette, Dragonette, Ltd., Los Angeles*
*Holly Eastman, Kentshire Antiques, New York*
*Elizabeth Feld, Hirschl & Adler, New York*
*Patrick Frémontier, Galerie Frémontier, Paris*
*Kathryn Gargolinski, Skinner, Inc., Boston*
*Bernd Goeckler, Bernd Goeckler Antiques, New York*
*Dan Harrison, H.M. Luther, New York*
*Carlton Hobbs, Carlton Hobbs, LLC, New York*
*Nicole Kapit, Newel, New York*
*Bernard Karr, Hyde Park Antiques, New York*
*Jean Karajian, Jean Karajian Gallery, New York*
*Murat Kupcu, Double Knot, New York*
*Rodrigo Rivero Lake, Rodrigo Rivero Lake Anticuario, Mexico City*
*Richard Lan, Martayan Lan Rare Books and Maps, New York*
*Sylvain Lévy-Alban, Sylvain Lévy-Alban Antiquités, Paris*
*Robert Lighton, British Khaki, New York*
*Conor Mahony, Chinese Porcelain Company, New York*
*Jim Marinaccio, Naga Antiques, New York*
*Mira Nakashima, George Nakashima Woodworker, New Hope, PA*
*Paul Provost, Christie's, New York*
*Yancey Richardson, Yancey Richardson Gallery, New York*

*Darius Sahkai, Darius Collection at Stark, New York*
*James Sansum, James Sansum Fine and Decorative Art, New York*
*Omri Schwartz, Nazmiyal Antique Rugs, New York*
*Susan Seidel, Susan Seidel, Inc., New York*
*Niall Smith, Niall Smith Antiques, New York*
*Colin Stair and Muffie Cunningham, Stair Galleries, Hudson, New York*
*Arlie Sulka, Lillian Nassau, New York*
*Tom Swope, Tom Swope Gallery, Hudson, New York*
*Spencer Throckmorton, Throckmorton Fine Art, New York*
*Elaine Whitmire, Sotheby's, New York*
*Gerard Widdershoven, Maison Gerard, New York*

## 1stdibs
*The peerless online marketplace where we go first for all things antique and vintage.*

## Donald Kaufman and Taffy Dahl
*whose brilliant paint palettes have brought so much beauty to our world.*

## The professionals who turn M (Group)'s visions into realities
*APF Master Frame makers*
*Carolyn Gregg Flowers*
*Cline Bettridge Bernstein Lighting Design*
*Diamint Upholstery*
*Hobbs, Inc.*
*Frank Keller, Art handler*
*Kelly Varnell Virgona Landscape Architects*
*Henry B. Urban Upholstery*
*Plant Specialists*
*St. Charles of New York*
*Stair Restoration*
*Stark Carpet*
*Uberto Ltd.*
*Vella Interiors*

## The New York Public Library
*The greatest public and research library system in the world, housed in one of New York's most beautiful buildings; free and welcoming to all who want to learn.*

*And last but not least…*

## Pointed Leaf Press
*Suzanne Slesin, the "Book Genius," and Stafford Cliff took my vision and, with Dominick Santise, made* Stuff *happen, with the help of the talented Regan Toews, Deanna Kawitzky, Marion D.S. Dreyfus, and Anita Tan. No one else could have done it*

*"Function in disaster, finish in style."*
*Miss Lucy Madiera*

## Carey Maloney—August 2012

**FRONT COVER** In Hermes Mallea's New York apartment, a long Chinese table serves as a work surface.

**BACK COVER** In a New York living room, an antique Japanese screen hangs above an eighteenth-century Chinese military treasure-trunk chest.

**CASE COVER** This detail is from an eighteenth-century tapestry that depicts Louis XIV's visit to the Gobelins workshop.

**ENDPAPERS** In Carey Maloney's New York dressing room, photographs and memorabilia create a vibrant collage.

**OPPOSITE HALF-TITLE** The bookshelves in Hermes Mallea's New York apartment have masks set into his book collection.

**OPPOSITE TITLE** In the 1944 movie *None But the Lonely Heart*, Cary Grant shows a painting to a wary Ethel Barrymore.

**PAGES 8-9** An early eighteenth-century tapestry, by the Studio of Leblond, after a painting by French artist Charles Le Brun, depicts the 1667 visit of Louis XIV to the Gobelins workshop.

**PAGES 10-11** A painting of the interior of a dealer's shop, either in an Indo-Chinese port or on the Coromandel Coast, with wares that include Chinese Export porcelain, paintings, and lacquered furniture.

**PAGES 12-13** A pen-and-ink drawing on paper dating from 1687 by seventeenth-century artist Sébastien Le Clerc illustrates an extraordinary Cabinet of Physics.

**PAGES 14-15** The eighteenth-century German neo-classical artist Johan Zoffany painted *The Tribuna of the Uffizi*, in which noblemen discuss sculptures and paintings.

**PAGES 16-17** This detail is from Mexican artist Diego Rivera's 1945 mural entitled *The Great City of Tenochtitlan*.

**PAGES 18-19** Carey Maloney is always on the hunt for esoteric, wonderful, and unusual things.

M (Group)
212-874-0773
www.mgrouponline.com

Inquiries should be addressed to:

Pointed Leaf Press, LLC.
136 Baxter Street, New York, NY 10013
www.pointedleafpress.com

Pointed Leaf Press is pleased to offer special discounts for our publications. We also create special editions and can provide signed copies upon request. Please contact info@pointedleafpress.com for details.

Printed in Malaysia for Imago
First edition
10 9 8 7 6 5 4 3 2 1
Library of Congress Control Number: 2012936440
ISBN: 978-0-9833889-8-2